RENEWALS: 691-4574

DATE DUE

FEB 18

GAYLORD

D1053384

The Black High School and Its Community

The Black High School and Its Community

WITHDRAWN
UTSA Libraries

Frederick A. Rodgers
University of Illinois

Lexington Books
D.C. Heath and Company
Lexington, Massachusetts
Toronto   London

Grateful acknowledgment is made for use of material reprinted from "Democratic Participation," by Sydney Verba, in volume no. 373 of THE ANNALS of the American Academy of Political and Social Science. Copyright 1967 by The American Academy of Political and Social Science.

Library of Congress Cataloging in Publication Data

Rodgers, Frederick A.
    The Black high school and Its community.

    Bibliography: p.
    Includes index.
    1. Negro high schools—North Carolina. 2. School integration—North Carolina. I. Title.
    LC2802.N8R62   373.756   74-21485
    ISBN 0-669-96818-8

Copyright © 1975 by D.C. Heath and Company.

Reproduction in whole or in part permitted for any purpose of the United States Government.

All rights reserved. No part of this publication may be reproduced or transmitted in any form or by any means, electronic or mechanical, including photocopy, recording, or any information storage or retrieval system, without permission in writing from the publisher. The provision of the United States Government constitutes the only exception to this prohibition. This work was prepared for the National Institute of Education, under research contract G-00-3-0218 authorized by the National Institute of Education. Since contractors performing research under Government sponsorship are encouraged to express their own judgment freely, the report does not necessarily represent the Department's official opinion or policy. Moreover, the contractor is solely responsible for the factual accuracy of all material developed in the report.

Published simultaneously in Canada.

Printed in the United States of America.

International Standard Book Number: 0-669-96818-8

Library of Congress Catalog Card Number: 74-21485

LIBRARY
University of Texas
At San Antonio

To my sons, Alex and Darryl,
and all black youth who
attend public schools

Contents

List of Tables

Preface

One of the critical problems facing public officials and laymen today is the formulation of policy for social services for individual citizens. Part of the difficulty is associated with the nature of the intended and unintended effects of policy directed at institutions established to serve certain social functions. The black high school experienced both the intended and hidden aspects of school desegregation policies. It is the intent of this book to show how knowledge of the relationship between policy and practice is crucial to one's understanding of how well social problems are met and resolved.

The focus of this book is directed on the black high school as an educational and social institution. It represents a composite view of the black high school based on official public data and the expressed perceptions of participants connected directly and indirectly with the ongoing activities of the institution. Data collected during the 1963-64 scholastic year were chosen as the base for reconstructing the functional and descriptive aspects of the black high school. The selection of this year was determined by the fact that the state (North Carolina) of our focus ceased to collect dual school data (separate data on black and white public schools) at the end of the 1963-64 scholastic year.

When the composite picture of the black high school was complete, the author directed attention to some changes for black and white students resulting from school desegregation that occurred after 1964. An attempt was made to describe how structural changes in schools have had a great impact not only on the institution in which they occur, but also on the attitudes and opportunities of those people who are part of that institution.

Acknowledgments

A project such as this requires the help of many people with many different areas of expertise, and it is impossible to thank them all personally. I therefore wish to thank the staff of the North Carolina Department of Public Instruction for providing the project staff with information on where to find data, with encouragement and support, and for the time they spent with us. I extend special thanks to Dr. H.T. Connor, Director of Research and Development, North Carolina State Department of Public Instruction, whose wide-ranging knowledge of North Carolina's educational system was invaluable. I also wish to thank Dudley E. Flood, Director of the Division of Human Relations; Marie Haigwood, Special Assistant for Elementary Education; Dr. Nile Hunt, Special Assistant for Secondary Education; Thelma Lennon, Director of the Division of Pupil Personnel Services; Philip Olmstead of the Division of Management Information Systems; and Dr. J.L. Pierce, Director of the Division of School Planning. Although we worked closely with the State Department of Public Instruction, this study in no way reflects their point of view. The conclusions are entirely my own.

I also wish to thank all the superintendents and principals who participated in this project, with special thanks to those who not only filled out long, detailed questionnaires but who also gave extra time for interviews. Thanks also go to the teachers, parents, students, and community leaders who provided us with much valuable information.

I also wish to thank the project staff and consultants who administered questionnaires, conducted interviews, and collected data from throughout North Carolina. Here special thanks go to Roosevelt Ellis, state coordinator (North Carolina) for the project, and Hattie Margaret Ellis, whose knowledge of North Carolina's education system and whose contacts throughout the state added greatly to the over-all quality of the study.

Special acknowledgments are due Susan Gonzo and Pamela Phillips, who assisted in conducting the research, and without whose untiring efforts and attention to detail the project could not have been completed. Lastly, special appreciation goes to Diane Campbell, who painstakingly typed and retyped the many versions of the manuscript.

In closing, I wish to say again that I am indebted to all those people whose encouragement, support, suggestions, and assistance helped make this project a reality. Furthermore, I wish to say that I take full responsibility for any errors or misinterpretations that may occur in the study.

1

Segregation, Desegregation, and Integration in Public Schools

Public schools for black children in North Carolina were instituted during the 1873-74 school year on a segregated basis.[1] The legal segregation of public schools for blacks in North Carolina existed until the Supreme Court's *Brown v. Board of Education* decision in 1954. In practice, segregated public schools for black children persisted in most North Carolina communities until the end of the 1963-64 school year.

The 1963-64 school year marked the end of an era, an institution, and a way of life in the delivery of educational services to the youth of North Carolina. This was the last year that the state of North Carolina collected data on a dual school system (basically one system for blacks and one system for whites, although there were separate Indian schools). This ended the ninety-year practice of collecting and presenting data on black and white schools separately. Thus, the 1964-65 school year marked the official beginning of a desegregated school system, even though many schools were attended exclusively by either blacks or whites for a few years after that time.

It is our interest here to document and analyze structural, curricular, and human experiences associated with segregated and desegregated schools in North Carolina as a basis for determining some of the *effects of policy on practice* in public schools. This effort is based on the contention that sharp changes in educational or social policy (in this case from segregated to desegregated schools) have profound impact on the staff, students, and programs in public schools and in the communities served. Even though policy changes are much more easily documented than resulting changes in practice, policy changes may be more difficult to associate with specific educational outcomes. This book focuses on the actual practices in the schools affected before and after the policy change of segregation to desegregation.

Formulation of Policy Boundaries

To document the relationship between policy and practice when applied to social problems, certain policy boundaries must be established to provide meaningful frames of reference and to facilitate analysis. For our purposes these policy boundaries include the operation of public black high schools in communities throughout North Carolina and the philosophical and moral positions suggested when citizens interact under the banners of segregation,

1

desegregation, and integration. In the first instance, public black high schools in North Carolina, we are providing a specific institutional boundary (the school and its activities) for analyzing policy and practice. In the second instance, segregation, desegregation and integration, we are providing general institutional boundaries that are primarily concerned with societal prerogatives, patterns, and practices. In both instances we are examining the "stateways" and "folkways" that influence the social functions of our basic institutions and, ultimately, the general well-being of our society.

Policy boundaries establish the domain of analysis and the behavior units and settings that can be utilized to collect data resulting from practices in social institutions. These boundaries also help one to understand how policy is determined by the moral values of the society and how practice is affected by institutions shaped by certain public policies. In part, this justifies conceptualizing segregation, desegregation, and integration as policy boundaries for the study of the public school experience of black youth.

Segregation as a Policy Boundary

Segregation has a long and persistent history in American life and practice. It has been used to deal with aspects of religion, race, sex, and age in terms of individual and group rights. At some points in our history, segregation as a policy boundary has been used to formulate public policy concerning the rights and privileges of defined groups such as blacks, Indians, and women. Over the years the basic direction has been toward eliminating public policy that creates and perpetuates the boundaries of segregation. In short, we have moved toward a public policy that sought to eliminate *de jure* segregation.

In a pluralistic society such as ours, segregation as a policy boundary serves to protect the rights and privileges of individuals and groups. This makes it possible for individuals and groups to form voluntary associations and pursue activities apart from other members in society. These individuals and groups have the right to include or exclude members on the basis of criteria of their own choice. This situation is the result of policies in the private sector. Public policy in the United States supports this type of segregation.

The point to be made here is that, while public policy imposed involuntarily on selected individuals is discriminatory and antidemocratic, public policy that allows selected individuals to voluntarily impose criteria for membership in selected groups is consistent with democratic practice.

Our concern here is with segregation as a public policy formulated to impose restrictions on selected groups against their will or perceived best interest. An example is the legal establishment of public schools on a racially segregated basis. This legal act set the stage for discrimination in the appropriation and allocation of resources to public schools used by different racial groups. In addition, the legal segregation of public schools set the stage for different socialization patterns and practices within each of the school systems used by the various groups. This notion of segregation as a policy boundary in terms of public education serves as one vantage point for viewing the black high school and its community.

Desegregation as Policy Boundary

When desegregation serves as a policy boundary, the legal restraints for selected group participation in public and private institutions are removed. Participation in social institutions under the banner of desegregation does not legally and morally exclude individuals on the basis of race or other arbitrarily chosen defining characteristics. As a policy boundary desegregation does not restrict nor does it ensure total involvement in social institutions. Desegregation provides a minimum structural arrangement for determining policy that deals with participation opportunities of individuals in different social institutions.

Desegregation suggests a very different pattern of institutional involvement, and of allocation, distribution, and utilization of resources—both human and material—than is the case with segregation. As a result of this, desegregation certifies and specifies the rights of individuals to participate in social institutions but does not determine the nature and quality of participation individuals will experience. The nature and quality of personal interaction in social institutions are often not explicitly denoted under the notion of desegregation (especially in terms of its operational implication).

It is entirely possible to have segregation within a social institution governed by the principle of desegregation. This situation is very evident when one views ability grouping in newly desegregated schools, or black studies programs in universities, or separate affirmative action programs to deal with special groups of individuals, or the leadership and decision-making structure of major social institutions. While desegregation as a policy boundary ensures the rights of individuals to participate in social institutions, it does not guarantee full participation across all levels and with regard to all issues. Desegregation supports the claims of individuals for access to social institutions, but it gives no assurance of individual attainment of rewards and privileges.

Integration as a Policy Boundary

Integration as a policy boundary is probably best thought of as a higher level of desegregation. Integration deals more with operational than with legal aspects of individual participation patterns. Under integration policy, individual participation in social institutions goes beyond legal and moral rights, because it deals with facets of participation across levels and issues affecting all activity. Integration fulfills both the letter and spirit of the intended policy. In comparison, desegregation is primarily concerned with the letter of the policy.

Integration deals with the nature and quality of individual participation in social institutions. Participation in this case suggests total involvement by individuals in accord with their ability to fulfill the role positions available. Interactions between individuals is open, and restrictions are based on personal choices and institutional needs and requirements. The primary determinant of individual participation is natural, not artifically imposed. Integration comes closest to meeting the major goals of a democratic society and providing equality of opportunity to participate fully in the various social institutions that serve our needs and define our culture. To date, integration as a policy boundary seems to affect practice more often when social institutions are segregated than when these institutions are desegregated.

Some Functional Implications of Segregation, Desegregation, and Integration

We have discussed briefly and generally some of the defining characteristics of segregation, desegregation, and integration as policy boundaries that govern the extent and nature of the participation individual group members experience in social institutions. Public institutions are the service extension of governments at various levels of involvement in our society. In this context public institutions serve two functions: they deliver necessary social services, and they provide opportunities for individuals to learn how to contribute to the conduct of social functions while realizing personal goals via meaningful participation. The use of segregation, desegregation, and integration as policy boundaries have different implications for different individuals who serve in, and are served by, different social institutions created by public policy guiding governmental action.

Questions concerning the use of segregation, desegregation, and integration as policy boundaries focus on patterns of involvement (Who makes the decisions? Who can participate and at what levels? Who is to be served? What are the appropriate role expectations?) and on allocation and utilization of resources (On what basis will resources be divided? What will be the tenure of support? Who can benefit directly and indirectly from support? What are the appropriate problems for pursuit? How much of the resources can be applied to a particular problem area? Who has priority claims on resources?).

When segregation is used as a policy boundary there is an attempt to provide a semblance of equality without equity in the creation and operation of social institutions. This can be readily demonstrated in the dual school system. Blacks were given the legal right to have and operate schools within the general guidelines and statutes of the state's school code much in the same way white schools were supposed to operate in fulfilling this public responsibility. In principle, as both groups were able to utilize public resources to carry out public policy and serve their respective communities, they were provided equal status. However, blacks were never provided with the same resources and absolute decision control to carry out the mandate to the extent that was possible in the white community. In short, equity for the two communities was not available in practice. According to Professor Charles S. Johnson: "There can be no group segregation without discrimination," and "in equity any segregation that is not mutual or voluntary is discrimination."[2]

The dual school system was public policy imposed on blacks involuntarily and on whites voluntarily and resulted in resource and support inequities for both groups: less of their fair share for blacks and for more than their fair share for whites. Segregation as a policy boundary tends to provide equality without equity. It therefore is discriminatory in its effects.

Some positive aspects of segregation are associated with opportunities to participate in, and make decisions concerning, the operation of social institutions. Segregation makes it possible for the members of the in group to participate fully in the total operation of the social institution for which they are responsible. Segregation made it possible for blacks to utilize the resources of their social institutions in ways that contributed directly and indirectly to the development and prosperity of the black community.

When desegregation is used as a policy boundary, there is an attempt to provide a semblance of equality and equity in the creation and operation of social institutions. While desegregation affirms the rights of individuals to participate equally and equitably, it does not guarantee that all will receive their fair share of the associated privileges. For example, desegregating dual school systems presumably allowed students, staff, and parents to use common resources and to participate fully in all activities and programs. However, the extent of participation is often based on factors that preclude the actual involvement of members of some groups. For instance, one way to eliminate opportunities for participation is to reduce the number of institutional role positions available. It is most unlikely that the least privileged group will be given power in the new organization. Therefore, they are in the least effective position to ensure participation at all levels in the social institution under consideration. Desegregation makes equality and equity possible but not necessarily a reality.

In terms of community development, desegregation makes it impossible for blacks to utilize social institutions directly to further their long-term goals and interests. Under desegregation the influence of social institutions on the positive development of black communities resulting from black initiatives is indirect at best. Under a policy of segregation, a certain amount of the resources were always made available, though inequitably, to support blacks in social institutions; desegregation gives blacks access to a greater amount of the resources but does not guarantee a given level of attainment. The way is still left open for blacks to continue to receive less than their fair share of the resources and in too many instances less than the share they received when they were operating under the banner of segregation.

When integration is used as a policy boundary, there is an attempt to provide equality and equity for all individuals in the creation and operation of social institutions. Integration not only affirms the rights of individuals to participate but seeks to ensure the reality and completeness of that participation. This pattern suggests that all people have the same opportunity to serve in, and to be served by, social institutions at all levels. Continuing with the dual school example, integration suggests that combining the two schools will extend the opportunity for all concerned both within and outside the social institution. Integration leads to personal interactions that are generalized across other areas in our society and contribute directly and indirectly to the development of the total community, thus benefiting all. Unfortunately, few instances of institutional integration fit this description. In some places, however, the trend is in the direction of integration. For example, entertainment and professional athletics are among the most integrated institutions we have in our society both in terms of participation and control. This trend is likely to continue and spread to other institutions as more favorable and meaningful integration experiences become common.

Separation and Participation

In a pluralistic society such as ours, with a number of easily identified ethnic and racial groups who rearrange themselves as subgroups on the basis of held beliefs, traditions, expectations and self-interest, separation for participation is the rule rather than the exception. This principle is operationally defined when such groups as the Greeks, Irish, Polish, Italians, Lithuanians, and Chinese choose to live in certain neighborhoods, join group associations, elect political representatives, and celebrate holidays that have common meaning for the whole group. In order to participate in social institutions with more specific functions, these groups further divide themselves into religious denominations, cooperatives, trade unions, political clubs, savings and loan associations, and other social group arrangements to pursue personal goals while conducting necessary social functions. Separation for participation is a salient characteristic of groups in all societies. This is especially the case in American society, where our population is pluralistic in a variety of ways and political system supports and encourages individual choice.

Our primary concern here is the way involuntary separations affect the participation of defined groups. In the main, public policy supports individual's and group's rights to separate voluntarily to participate in political activity and pursue personal and social goals. For the most part, this is done on an equal basis across groups. However, in some notable instances public policy forces involuntary separation on certain well-defined groups, such as blacks, native Americans, women, and the aged. While in these instances, the participation arena is defined by public policy, the nature and form of the resulting participation patterns are determined by the focus group and the function of the social institution in question. Even though involuntary separation limits external effects of a group's participation influence, the internal effects of participation contribute individual and community accomplishment, growth, and development in ways that benefit society at large. Just because involuntary separation makes it possible for positive participation experiences to occur in selected social institutions, one should not conclude that a democratic society can maintain itself if it continues to employ public policy that creates involuntary separations for purposes of participation. The over-all effect of such a policy is negative.

In the final analysis, the question of participation, whether voluntary or involuntary, has to be considered in terms of our democratic value structure.

The most notable of the problems that have been neglected are those that concern the functioning of our social and political institutions. To the extent that these institutions have promoted health, deterred crime, and the like, their achievements [become the subject of another focus]. But we also care about *how* we combine our efforts to achieve our goals, about our loyalty toward our institutions, about our attitudes toward each other, and about the implications of our social and political institutions for the future of the nation. However good our health or high our incomes, we would not be satisfied with institutions that failed to respect individual rights, allow democratic participation, provide congenial group affiliations, or insure the survival and orderly development of our society.[3]

We must evaluate participation in the broader context of democratic values if we are to draw any conclusions about the ultimate effect of participation on the various forms of separation. When participation is viewed in this context its significance to total society becomes apparent.

Another important aspect of separation and participation must deal with the nature of participation in the context of a democratic society. The definition of democratic participation under which we labor "refers to the processes by which citizens influence or control those who make major decisions affecting them."[4] In terms of democratic participation, voluntary separation enables individuals and groups to affect social and political arrangements for their mutual benefit that are both external and internal to the social institution with which they are involved. On the other hand, involuntary separation weakens the external effects of participation, though the internal effects of such participation may be positive to the individuals involved and ultimately to the general society.

In considering this problem it must be remembered:

"Participatory democracy" is not an all-or-nothing thing; every society allows some means of participation for some citizens; and this society is run on the basis of equal participation by all citizens. The United States is one of the happy few nations of the world which have passed many of the traditional crises of participation—for example, the incorporation of a multiplicity of ethnic groups into democratic politics. But the problems of participation are never solved once and for all. As societies change and new problems arise, issues of participation come to the fore again, as they do in the current racial crisis.[5]

As a policy boundary, desegregation suggests a very different pattern of involvement and allocation and utilization of resources than does segregation. On the question of institutional involvement, segregation separates individuals but does not try to control the pattern of interactions within the institution in question.

Issues surrounding participatory democracy both within social institutions and the general society will continue to require systematic study and reassessment. Because it is necessary for some individuals and groups to separate for participation, more attention has to be directed toward how these patterns affect participatory democracy.

It should be remembered that the issues of participation are basically concerned with

who participates, about what and how? There is an acute crisis of participation in contemporary United States because all three issues are being raised at once: new people want to participate, in relation to new issues, and in new ways. The question of who ought to participate has been raised most strikingly by Southern Negroes; but in colleges, students want to participate and in welfare agencies, clients want some voice. At the same time, participation is demanded in relation to a wider range of issues or governmental activities: the subjects of administrative programs demand chances to participate within such programs; parents demand more voice in school planning; the students demand more voice in deciding what they are taught. . . . Indeed, in relation to almost every substantive area of political controversy in contemporary America there is a parallel controversy over who participates in decisions relevant to that area.[6]

Participation patterns and issues will continue to be a factor in public policy decisions. It is our intent to study some of these issues within the context of ongoing social institutions such as the public black high school.

Desegregation and Alienation

At the onset of the desegregation of social institutions some individuals experience a degree of alienation. Members of groups that had less power are more likely to feel alienated in newly desegregated social institutions, especially if they are not made to think that they are involved totally at all levels in the activities and decision making guiding these activities. This situation is exaggerated by the fact that both groups had previously been members of social institutions (dual school systems) and participated fully in the activity and decision-making structure at all levels of involvement. Care should be exercised not to attach too much negative valence to some alienation that results from desegregation.

Some degree of alienation and disunity is acceptable in a society that values individual freedom, and the alienated may be creative and bring about reforms which benefit society as a whole. But if alienation becomes so pervasive that all sense of community is lost, the result can be disaster.[7]

The level and extent of individual alienation must be a continuing concern if desegregation as a public policy is to achieve the social goals expected while maintaining consistency with democratic values.

The relationship between desegregation and alienation must also be viewed within the context of the total society.

The degree of alienation also depends on the functioning of all the social groups in the society. A person may be alienated because of the failure of his family, the shortcomings of his neighborhood, the lack of a congenial club, or the policies of the National Government.[8]

Any analysis of desegregation and alienation in a particular social institution such as the school must take into account other pressures that characterize our society and affect the emotions of individuals toward themselves and others. A greater coverage of the relevant aspects of desegregation and alienation in terms of a specific manifestation in public schools and general occurrence in society will be discussed in detail later in the book.

Self-Determination of Minority
Groups in Integrated Public Schools

As minority children are integrated into public schools in greater numbers, their personal characteristics will take on greater significance as they seek to participate fully in the schools' programs and activities. Integrated schools work to the extent that all students act to utilize the available resources for their own purposes. The equality of opportunity suggested by integrated schools is a two-way street. Students in integrated schools have the right of access to available resources and the responsibility to pursue available experiences. This condition of integrated education is particularly tough on the minority student. In the first place, the minority student is more likely to feel a sense of powerlessness in, and distance from, the altered social atmosphere of integrated schools. This makes it less likely that a minority student will assert himself and join different kinds of social group arrangements that lead to more extensive and qualitative involvement in all of the school's programs and activities. To become more involved, the minority student must have a well-defined sense of self-determination, even if it means venturing outside his usual psychological field (primary reference group). Often this means that the minority student who takes this step will be alone and without support from his friends or others. Without this self-determination, minority students have too many factors against them to acquire the educational opportunities available to them in integrated schools. This must be taken into account when one attempts to assess the influence of integrated schools on the educational experience of minority students.

2 Purpose of the Study

The formerly all-black high school had both direct and indirect functions in developing leadership skills and providing apprenticeship opportunities for students, parents, and staff. It is important to examine the black high school as it previously existed as a basis for describing and documenting its positive contributions and the associated facets and interrelationships to the black community in particular and the larger community in general. Many of these facets and interrelationships cannot be recaptured now by simply looking at problems and issues that have arisen in the totally integrated school system and attempting to reconstruct the common operational structure of the all-black high school. The black high school was a world of its own, with its own dynamic quality and its own ecological structure. It played a definite and specific role in the lives of people who touched it and were touched by it. By examining what did exist, it is possible to spotlight changes that have occurred in the community as a result of the removal of the black high school as a viable, dynamic, and pervasive force from the total structure of the community it served. This examination makes it possible to:

1. describe the structure of the black high school and discuss the black high school as a historic phenomenon in the public education of black citizens;
2. use official data to document and describe the formal structure of the black high school;
3. make professional educators aware of the great influence that leadership and membership experiences can have on students;
4. provide a new approach to viewing the school as a socializing agency that had different effects on the futures of different students;
5. discuss the practices and procedures that enabled the black high school system to make positive contributions to the community;
6. point out previously ignored functions of the school and assess the importance of these to later individual success as well as to the development of the larger community; and
7. establish whether or not the methodology employed to highlight these qualitative aspects of the black high school experience is valid.

During the last half of the 1960s, there was an increased awareness among black citizens, primarily in northern urban cities, of the increasing deficiencies in achievement demonstrated by black children attending public schools. The achievement of black students in these areas worsened at each grade level from year to year and as each class moved to the next grade level. In addition, a growing percentage of black students were getting into difficulty with school officials, and many of them were dropping out before completing their public school education. As the many deficiencies affecting the education of black youth were counted and noted in a variety and number of urban areas located in states outside the South, there was increased agitation for control over the operation of schools by the parents of the children served. This was the period when community control became the political ideal in most urban areas outside the South.

Community control advocates argued that a smaller percentage of the country's white population were urban dwellers and an increasingly larger percentage of that urban population (central city) was black.[1] The staff and personnel in schools located in these cities failed to reflect the composition of the students served. Consequently, with the increasing percentage of black children there was not a similar increase in staff who came from a similar background and who had the psychological, sociological, emotional, and knowledge set to contribute effectively to the education of these children. As a result of this, so the argument goes, the achievement level of black children lagged behind all others, and the personal relationship that motivated them to learn was not possible with teachers who were not black. From all of this it was concluded that schools attended by black children should be staffed and administered by members from their own group who cared for them as persons and believed in their ability to achieve as learners. This change would ensure the motivation of black children and would improve their image of themselves and increase their level of achievement.

On the surface, the community control argument allows for improvement of the achievement and self-image of black children by using staff and personnel from the same group. It places the burden of positive change on the shoulders of the teachers themselves, who exercise their judgment in fulfilling the roles expected of them and required in schools. Primarily, it leaves intact the institutional structure, patterns of operation, types of resources deployed, and approaches to instruction. To expect great change by only manipulating people and not their environment is to place too much weight on one side of the equation affecting achievement and personal satisfaction in schools. However, it is difficult to counter such arguments with evidence, since it has never been tried in northern cities and since the facts suggest community control as the logical and reasonable solution to a persistent problem. The quest for supportive evidence is in part responsible for the study of all-black schools in areas where schools were legally separated into segregated units.

After some thinking on the problem of community control of schools by black parents and professional staff in northern cities, it is clear that some evidence should be presented to determine whether it is a "people-to-people" problem, or a problem of institutional structure, or a combination of the two. What is needed is an example of schools where black professional staff had complete operational control over the education of black children in publicly supported schools. The only place where this appears to have been a practice was in southern or border states where the dual school system was a legally sanctioned approach to education. Black schools in dual school systems were staffed, managed, and maintained by black professional staff. Given that reality, a study of the dynamic and static components of these schools should reveal evidence gathered from those who attended the various schools that would shed some light on the claims made by supporters of community control. An additional reason for looking at the all-black high school is to observe the effects of its educational efforts with black students on the development of the black community.

North Carolina as a Study Site

North Carolina was selected as a study site for a variety of reasons. As a state, North Carolina probably operated one of the best black school systems under the dual system of education. This conclusion is based on the comparatively high level of state support for black higher education in North Carolina. Table 2-1 reveals that 66 percent of all black college students in North Carolina were enrolled in black state-supported institutions in 1963-64 and that there were five black state-supported institutions of higher education in the state. No other state had more state-supported colleges for black students than North Carolina, even though Louisiana and Arkansas had a larger percentage of black students educated in state-supported institutions. In absolute numbers, only Louisiana had more black students enrolled in state-supported colleges in 1963-64, and only Texas had more black students enrolled in all institutions in 1970. It should also be noted that there was only a 5.7 percent spread between the percentage of blacks in the population and the percentage of blacks in the college population in the state. While North Carolina ranks fifth among these states in per capita income, in 1971 it ranked fourth in providing college spaces for black students in proportion to their representation in the total state population. Since it is reasonable to assume that the presence of higher education opportunities was the key to staffing black high schools in the segregated system, North Carolina proved to be one of the leaders among the states that had an official dual school system. This lent added support to selecting North Carolina as the state to provide the data base for this book.

In addition, North Carolina has been a relatively progressive state and, as such, probably mirrors closely how the black high school operated optimally given the conditions under which it existed. Also, the writer was born and attended public grade schools and a publicly supported college in North

Table 2-1
Selected Comparisons of Educational Statistics Among States That Comprised the Confederacy

States	Percent of Black Population				1963-64 Affiliation of Black Colleges			1963-64 Enrollment in State-Supported Black Post-Secondary Institutions			1970 Black Enrollment in All Post-Secondary Institutions			1970 Percentage Difference Between Population and Enrollment			Per Capita Income 1970 (Black and White)	
	1960		1970			Local Govern-	Pri-vate and Church									Percent		
	Percent	Rank	Percent	Rank	State	ment	Related	No.	Percent	Rank	No.	Percent	Rank	Diff.	Rank	Covered	Rank	Income
Alabama	30	4	26.2	4	2		9	2,455	33	10	14,944	18.7	5	−7.5	7	71	9	2,828
Arkansas	22	7	18.3	8	1		2	2,242	73	11	5,877	14.8	11	−3.5	2	81	10	2,742
Florida	18	9	15.3	10	2	9	2	3,342	43	7	12,740	9.3	7	−6.0	6	61	2	3,584
Georgia	28	5	25.9	5	3		7	3,195	43	8	13,641	17.1	6	−8.8	9	66	4	3,277
Louisiana	32	3	29.8	3	2		2	8,752	84	1	17,773	20.7	3	−9.1	10	69	6	3,065
Mississippi	42	1	36.8	1	4	2	10	4,299	57	4	15,383	28.9	4	−7.9	8	79	11	2,561
North Carolina	24	6	22.2	6	5	1	7	8,424	66	2	20,887	16.5	2	−5.7	4	74	5	3,188
South Carolina	35	2	30.5	2	1		7	2,519	44	9	8,383	16.6	10	−13.9	11	54	8	2,908
Tennessee	16	10	15.8	9	1		7	4,200	53	5	11,885	12.7	9	−3.1	1	80	7	3,051
Texas	12	11	12.5	11	2	2	9	7,274	65	3	22,282	7.8	1	−4.7	3	62	3	3,515
Virginia	21	8	18.5	7	1		4	3,884	53	6	12,121	12.7	8	−5.8	5	69	1	3,586

Carolina. He was personally acquainted with key informants and the conditions under which they worked in several counties and major cities.

The Black High School and
Community Development

In studying the relationship between the black high school and its community, it is necessary to view the student, the school, and the community as components of a complex interdependent system. This is particularly true in the case of black high schools in black communities in North Carolina.

To justify this assumption, one has to establish the kind of role these high schools played. Educational literature is presently filled with studies that set out to measure black students' performances against some standard of behavior or another and that conclude, if the results differ from the norm, that the difference is the result of some kind of social pathology, disorder at home, or unprofessional or unethical practices at school. These conclusions are not based on any observation of home life or community environment. To truly study the effects that school has on students, it is necessary to look at schools in the larger context of the child's total environment, his community. If a child's perform- ance and expectations in school are not, in fact, determined solely by his school, then the school is not a closed system, not an isolated environment, but part of some other, larger system. For black high schools in North Carolina, this system consists of the black community. This community can be defined as:

1. those who are directly involved in the schools, such as teachers, principals, and other school employees and students;
2. those indirectly involved in the school, such as parents of students, younger siblings; and
3. those even less directly involved in the school, including those who attended the school and who still live in the area, and those who never attended, but make use of its facilities or attend and/or support school activities, such as sports and other extracurricular activities.

Membership in a particular school community is limited really only by two factors: race and location. Any black in the area served by the black high school can be considered a member of that community. Some members merely play a more integral part in the community and in the school than others.

Black high schools in North Carolina served fairly small communities. Ninety-eight percent were located in towns of less than 50,000 or in rural areas. Until recently, teaching and other official school positions were about the only high-status white-collar jobs open to blacks in the South. Other blacks in the community, aside from the few prosperous small businessmen and farmer-owners, were tenant farmers or were employed as manual laborers and domestic help. Black high schools and those holding high positions within the school were usually at the apex of the social structure. This was particularly apparent in the smaller communities, where the black high school might well be the largest—sometimes the only—social and financial enterprise going: more blacks would work at the school than at any other single place. In these cases, it is obvious that the school had a central role in the functioning of the community. Even in larger cities, where there might be more than one black high school, the school played an important role both economically and in terms of status, for here, too, the school provided more white-collar, high-paying jobs than anywhere else in the city or large town. Structurally, then, the black high school was extremely important in the black community.

From 1873, when black public schools were first established in North Carolina, until 1907, there were no high schools. The school term was something less than four months, the "Three Rs" were the main subject matter, and school plants were tiny and understaffed. Few people felt that education was very important. But by the time that black high schools were beginning to be phased out of existence in North Carolina in the 1960s, schools were expected not only to teach reading, writing, and arithmetic, but were also expected to teach vocational skills, reinforce social and moral values, and provide extracurricular activities.[2] The school year was nine months by that time, and school plants and staff were sizable.

The man who headed this important community structure, the principal, was the man who ran the school and, in many cases, the black community. His influence in community affairs was almost without exception great. He was, therefore, central in community life and was indeed more knowledgeable about what was going on than anyone else. Also, as head of the black high school, he had a role in the white power structure as well. This usually put him in the position of knowing more about the larger community than any other black in the black community. He was often the only black with whom influential members of the white community had anything approaching professional contact. For an accurate description of what the black high school was like and what roles it played, it is, therefore, essential to take a close look at the man who was so central to the functioning of the high school and to study the roles he played. When we say that the high school played a major role in the functioning of the community and in its development, this implies that the principal of the black high school played a major role in the functioning and development of his community because of the importance of his role in the school.

Goals and Limitations

Most educational studies have suffered from what is known as the redundancy syndrome: they have attempted to use student behavior as the basis for identifying and describing the total school environment, overlooking the fact that students are not at all the only factor that enters into creating this environment. Therefore, their behavior cannot be seen as explaining their behavior, since this is obviously redundant and tautological. Many other factors besides students affect student school life and this book attempts to identify and use as sources these other factors.

Serious limitations can be associated with our goals and the nature of the available data. There has been an attempt to describe the black high school in North Carolina as fully as possible and, in doing so, to indicate its role in community development in North Carolina. The effort was limited by the fact that such schools no longer exist and by the very nature of observing human institutions. No two schools can ever be exactly the same, since to start with they do not have the same people as students, staff, etc., nor are they located in the same time and place. The view presented here has not established a pure model of the black high school and its role in community development in North Carolina because it is simply impossible to control all the variables to the point where it can be said that this is a totally accurate, objective description. The best that can be hoped for is to attempt to give the most accurate picture possible.

To achieve this a demographic display of the black high school over a period of time has been presented, making it possible to describe some of the factors that shaped the structure and operation of the black high school (Appendix B). Once a reasonable description of the structure and operation of the black high school is available through the use of demographic data, it is possible to derive at least a partial picture of the total environment of the black high school as it existed. This is one part of our study. The other part attempts to utilize information gained from students, staff, parents, and other citizens to provide the qualitative aspect of the black high school and what made it unique.

3

A Historical Perspective

Public support of common schools for white youth has been a continuing political issue in North Carolina since the end of the American Revolution. The Revolution created an intense hatred of any form of "taxation without representation," and Noble indicates that North Carolinians

emerged from the long years of that war victorious and more determined than ever to resist taxation in any form, and for any purpose whatever, it if could be avoided in any way. And so it was that, when the public mind turned seriously and anxiously to the task of creating a fund that would yield annually enough revenue to place an elementary school within easy reach of every white child in the state, the great object with our lawmakers was how to accomplish this result without having to resort to laying a public school tax.[1]

Given this general hostility to taxation, it is easy to see why public schooling had a long uphill climb in North Carolina. Fortunately for the advocates of public schooling, internal improvement had been actively promoted by every North Carolina governor.

The subject of internal improvements has always been a popular one in North Carolina, and it is a fact that education and internal improvements were advocated with equal force and favor in practically every governor's message sent to the legislature during the nineteenth century prior to the Civil War. The same liberal spirit of expansion and growth that promoted and championed the one, promoted and championed the other.[2]

The development of the state's resources and the strengthening of the public schools still remains a strong commitment and political force in North Carolina.

Sometime around 1823 the North Carolina legislature, in an attempt to devise a means for creating a public school fund without resorting to taxation, passed a bill authorizing the state treasurer to issue treasury notes. Some state officials and citizens felt that the proceeds of the notes could be used as the foundation of a permanent school fund that would provide the financial support required for initiating common schools throughout the state. Even though this attempt and related legal moves failed to win public or legislative approval, the seeds were sown, and support for public schools showed strong and hardy growth from that period onward. After many hard battles, the first law providing financial support for public schools in North Carolina was passed on December 22, 1825. According to one source,

Charles A. Hill, a member of one committee on education in the Senate, reported a bill to create a fund for the support of common schools. It was called "An Act to Create a Fund for the Establishment of Common Schools," and on January 4, 1826, it passed the Senate and became law. It is generally called "The Literary Fund Law of 1825."[3]

Even though The Literary Fund Law of 1825 referred to providing public support for the education of white children, the operational specifications of that law formed the basis for the first conflict over how black children in North Carolina would be covered by such funding of public schools and ultimately how they would be educated in them.

At this time (1825) the involvement of blacks in public education was indirect at best. Ironically, federal policy initiated the political conflict within the state of North Carolina that first raised the issues surrounding black involvement in public education. This politically touchy situation was created by an act of the U.S. Congress that gave general support to states providing public education.

In 1836 an Act of Congress directed that the surplus remaining in the Treasury of the United States on January 1, 1837, should be deposited with such of the states in proportion to their representation in the Senate and the House of Representatives, as would comply with the terms specified in the Act. The terms were such as to make the amount deposited with the state merely a loan to be returned when called for by the general government. The amount thus received by North Carolina was $1,433,757.39.[4]

Once received by North Carolina, these federal funds for public schools were to be distributed by the Literary Fund. The combination of "receiving funds in proportion to congressional representation" and "distribution of these funds to local areas via a state agency" set the stage for the drama that still rages around the public education of black and white children in the public schools in North Carolina and in the nation as a whole.

The seeds of conflict surrounding the issue of public education of black children had been sown, but the first confrontation awaited the passage of a resolution offered in the state senate by Alfred Dockery on December 6, 1938, "instructing the committee on education to inquire into the expediency of distributing the income from the Literary Fund among the counties of the state, in proportion to their federal population, for the purpose of educating the children of the indigent poor."[5] This resolution was later expanded in a proposal by H.G. Spruill, senator from Washington and Tyrrel counties, when "he struck at the question of common schools from the broad and statesmanlike viewpoint of public education for all children at public expense with no reference whatever to either the rich or the poor."[6] Senator Spruill's resolution changed the conception of public school education in North Carolina with the inclusion of the phrase "all children." One other far-reaching aspect of Senator Spruill's resolution was an additional requirement suggesting the passage of a law that would send some sort of teacher into about 1250 schools, no one of which would be more than four miles from the center of the district. That law ultimately provided the foundation for the structure of elementary public schools in North Carolina. The present school system in North Carolina owes its beginnings to the forceful ideas expressed by Senator Spruill but shared by many.

The first free common school law was enacted in North Carolina in January 1839. This law was entitled "An Act to Divide the Counties of the State into School Districts and for Other Purposes" and established the system of public instruction that helped to pave the way for building a statewide structure for the education of North Carolina's youth. The act authorizing public instruction gained strength when a school tax bill was passed during the same year on August 8, 1839. It is noteworthy that the people of North Carolina, who hated any form of taxation with a passion, voted to provide "free countywide common schools at public expense" the first time they were given the opportunity. This concern for the interests of children in North Carolina has prevailed and influenced the direction and advancement of public schools for the public good.

One of the points regarding the common schools that profoundly affected the legislature, and consequently the political process, dealt with the method to be used to distribute state funds to local schools; which caused great conflict between counties with widely varying black populations. During each session of the state legislature from 1836 through 1851 efforts to change the method of distributing funds according to federal population were mounted with great resolve, but the opponents were always unsuccessful. In 1836 when the federal treasury was authorized to distribute funds for the support of local educational efforts on the basis of state representation in Congress, North Carolina showed a white population of 484,870 and a black population of 268,549. Given this situation, the state of North Carolina, on the basis of its total population, was to receive money from the federal treasury in part based on the number of black slaves "not one of whom would ever have one cent of public money spent on him for any kind of education."[7] However, the issues and principles brought into being by the existence of the federal act of 1836 probably contributed greatly to the 1954 decision by the Supreme Court to provide "equal education to all children" regardless of race, creed, or color.

The public schools in North Carolina experienced a steady growth in size and influence during their early existence. By 1857, there were 3500 school districts with at least one schoolhouse in each district. The combined school districts enrolled 150,000 of the 220,000 children of school age in the state. There were around 11,000 children enrolled in colleges, academies, and private schools. Some 27,000 children of school age had completed their common school education, and 2000 more were being taught either at home or in Sunday school. By 1857, 2256 teachers had been issued teaching certificates, 214 of whom were women. From these meager statistics it is evident that the public school system in North Carolina had made great strides in eighteen short years.

Another point of interest is that the average monthly teacher's salary in 1858 ($28.00) was second only to that of Massachusetts.[8] It is evident that North Carolina placed a great emphasis early in obtaining and attracting good teachers. They were willing to pay some of the highest salaries available to members of that profession in any state. In addition, North Carolina paid their female teachers almost as much as their male counterparts, not the practice in most places.

The Early Education of Blacks in North Carolina

The earliest date that plans for the public education of black children appear to have been officially initiated was October 2, 1865, when the constitutional convention met in Raleigh. On the same day a group of prominent black men met and drafted a statement to be presented to the convention, as a preparatory step for its presentation to the state legislature, which was slated to assemble in November of the same year. This statement requested the passage of laws that would prove helpful in dealing effectively with their new freedom and in providing the education their children would require to participate fully as citizens in the functioning of the state. The statement formulated by these black men was presented to the convention, which adopted a resolution directing Governor Holden to appoint a three-man commission to study the situation. This commission made its report to the state legislature on January 22, 1866.

It declared "persons of color to be citizens of the state" and that they ought to have conferred upon them "all privileges of white persons in conducting their suits, and the mode of trial by jury." It urged the legitimization of colored children born during the days of slavery, took ground for the repeal of laws that had been enacted from time to time in order to make certain distinctions between whites and colored persons," and in a very comprehensive manner presented and discussed much legislation deemed by them to be necessary to give freed men equal rights as citizens with white persons before the law. Of special note is the fact that the report recommended that a colored apprentice be placed "on the same footing with a white one."[9]

This statement of the equality of the races before the law reflects public willingness immediately following the Civil War to support fair treatment of the freedman. This trend in public opinion could have led to the provision of equal education for black children, which would have enabled them to qualify for active participation as citizens of the state. However, many factors combined to suppress this development.

The Civil War had completely depleted the resources used by the state to support public schools for white children. The destruction left citizens of the state of North Carolina with little capacity to reopen even these schools. Coupled with this was the fact that, for the first time,

white people were confronted with the thought of the possibility and probability of having to provide for the education of thousands of colored children recently set free from the bonds of slavery. Tradition, belief that the Negro was incapable of being educated, and the recollection of the fact that up to within a very few months before, it was a misdemeanor to teach him to read—all these facts stood in the way of many white leaders being willing to provide common school instruction for the children of ex-slaves.[10]

Even so, most whites in the immediate post-Civil War period recognized that citizenship rights had to be granted to blacks.

It is important to note that the law governing the obligation of the employer or the local community to white orphans provided the basic foundation for a law governing the education of some black children.

The destitute white orphan boy or girl, under the mandate of the law, had to be taught to read and write and also taught a trade, and, finally, the conscience of a Christian state assumed, in the School Law of 1838-39, the additional obligation to provide for the teaching of *all* white boys and girls rich or poor, at least the rudiments of an "English education."[11]

This law is a basic expression of fair treatment and positive help for those who could not act independently to cope with their unfortunate situation and could not contribute without some aid to the social functioning of their community and the state. Many local practices and procedures evolved in trying to implement this law for the white children of the state until it was stated in a more specific and explicit form in the Code of 1854:

The master or mistress shall provide for the apprentice diet, clothes, lodging, and accommodations fit and necessary; and such as are white, shall teach or cause to be taught to read and write, and the elementary rules of arithmetic; and at the expiration of every apprenticeship, shall pay to each apprentice, six dollars, and furnish him a new suit of clothes and a new Bible.[12]

During the legislative session of 1865-66, at the suggestion of the commission appointed by Governor Holden, a law was passed to strike out the phrase "such as are white." Not only was this the first piece of educational legislation passed after the Civil War, it legally equalized treatment of the black apprentice with that of the white.

It is important to note that the law allowing the education of the black apprentice was passed by members of the legislature who had been leaders prior to the Civil War. In that sense, long-term white political leaders from the state of

North Carolina voluntarily initiated the means for educating black youth in the state. The act striking out the white clause in the Code of 1854 was ratified March 10, 1866.

The legislation ratified in 1866 governing the education of black children gives the impression that the white citizens of North Carolina not only readily participated in providing the legal basis for the public education of black youth but that they dutifully followed that law. There is little reason to believe that this was the case, since the subsequent development of a system for the education of black youth took a wholly different turn in later years.

Noble concludes that the problem of the public education of black youth would have been solved by white southern leaders had they been left alone to pursue the course outlined in the legislation passed in 1866. However, what Noble considered a "solution" to the problem is, in his own words, "free public education of all colored children in colored public schools," implying that he gave little thought to the solution of the problem of permitting black children to attend existing public schools with white children. Since there was little money left after the Civil War for the public education of white children, it was unrealistic indeed to conclude that the white citizens of North Carolina were ready to build and operate public schools for black children during that period. Given those factors, providing public education for black children at public expense immediately following the Civil War might have been only an outside possibility if the children had been permitted to attend existing public schools instead of the near improbability it was, when it was made dependent on the establishment of new schools for black children. This proved to be an important consideration in the early decisions that shaped the foundations of the public school system that was to serve black children.

The Beginnings of the Dual School System

From the beginning, both black and white natives of North Carolina generally opposed any attempt to provide public education for black and white children in the same school building. Even though some advocated it, there was no serious attempt to achieve "integrated" education immediately following the Civil War. If, in fact, black and white citizens were generally opposed to their children attending the same school, why should this have become an issue that required the establishment of a dual school system by law rather than by practice, as had been the case in northern states, immediately after the Civil War? It appears that the fight over the issue of integrated common school education in local areas arose as a result of the efforts of conservative white lawmakers to pass amendments to keep separate and distinct the public education of white and black races by constitutional provision. For very good reasons, far-sighted black and white lawmakers felt that it would be a mistake to write into the constitution race distinctions that would become "organic law," insuring poor services for black youth and, over the long haul, harming the total development and prosperity of the state.

On the surface it appears that conservative whites were most concerned with fostering "social equality" in segregated schools. Therefore, a legal provision in the constitution would specify the status of both groups regarding public education in their respective schools. One of the most effective spokesmen against this view was J.W. Hood, the black legislator from Cumberland County, who asserted:

There will undoubtedly be separate schools in this state wherever it is possible, because both parties will demand it. My experience has been that the colored people in this state generally prefer colored preachers, when other things are equal, and I think the same will be found to be true respecting teachers. As the whites are in the majority in this state, the only way we can hope to have colored teachers is to have separate schools. And with all due respect to the noble self-sacrificing devotion that white teachers from the North have shown to the cause of the ignorant and despised colored people in the South—without detracting one iota from the amount of gratitude we owe them for that genuine philanthropy which has enabled them to bear up amid the contempt and ostracism that has been heaped upon them—I must be permitted to say that it is impossible for white teachers, educated as they necessarily are in this country, to enter into the feelings of colored pupils as the colored teacher does.[13]

It is clear from Hood's statement that there was little, if any, reason to be concerned about black children attending or wanting to attend schools with whites that would have warranted having it prohibited by the constitution. Politically, not having it in writing would seem to have provided the greatest protection for black citizens' legal right to public education. At the same time, individual localities would have been free to make arrangements conforming to the social practices of the area in question.

It was also evident from Hood's remarks that he was concerned both about the informal and formal aspects of black children's schooling. He did not believe that white teachers could or would provide adequate positive psychological support to make black children feel worthy and competent as human beings. His statement was the first official recognition that *the interests of black children might be better served by black teachers teaching in schools established for blacks.* It was Hood's contention that the idea of white superiority was too firmly implanted in white teachers to keep them from revealing it to black children through daily contact in class.

I do not believe that it is good for our children to eat and drink daily the sentiment that they are naturally inferior to the whites, which they do in three-fourths of all the schools where they have white teachers. There are numbers of colored people who really think that they are naturally inferior to white people. Nothing tries me more than to hear a black man make this admission; and yet they cannot be expected to do otherwise, when they learn it as they learn their letters, and it grows with their growth and strengthens with their strength. Taking this view of the case, I shall always do what I can to have colored teachers for colored schools. This will necessitate separate schools as a matter of course, wherever it is possible, not by written law, but by mutual consent and the law of interest. For this very reason I am opposed to putting it in the organic law. Make this distinction in your organic law and in many places the white children will have good schools at the expense of the whole people, while the colored people will have none or but little worse than none. If the schools are to be free at all, the colored children will be insured good schools in order to keep them out of white schools. This is all we ask, this we expect to contend for. I have expressed my objection time and again to the words white and black being put in this constitution.[14]

It is evident that even from the time the first plans were laid out for the public education of black children, many black spokesmen had no desire for their children to be educated with and by whites. However, they were opposed to giving separate education legal sanction in the state constitution. This issue endured to plague parties of both persuasions until the Supreme Court decision of 1954.

Even though black lawmakers and some of their white supporters were violently opposed to making blackness and whiteness the basis for a constitutional amendment providing for separate public education to the state's children, they finally agreed to a compromise. In order to move the legislation forward, W.J.T. Hayes, a black legislator from Halifax County, offered the following resolution, adopted on March 16, 1868: "Resolved, That it is the sense of this Convention that intermarriages and illegal intercourse between the races should be discountenanced, and the interests and happiness of the two races would be best promoted by the establishment of separate schools."[15] This proved to be the first crack in the front holding out against legally mandating separate schools for black and white youth. Even though the resolution paved the way for a dual school system, it was a true compromise, for black people won control of their schools and white people did not have to attend school with blacks. This situation led Noble to conclude:

So far as separate schools for the races were concerned, this resolution was merely an expression of opinion as to the best way of promoting the interests and happiness of the two races, and was not regarded by the Conservatives as an answer to their contention that, under the proposed constitution, mixed schools were not only not prohibited but actually authorized.[16]

Even though the legislature had acted to bring free public school education to black children in North Carolina, there were many obstacles. For the most part there was a general objection among most whites to the education of blacks at public or even the blacks' own expense. In addition, there were never enough teachers to teach black children, and what teachers there were often faced the problem of a general lack of facilities for holding classes. On many occasions white teachers who agreed to teach black children were harassed and ostracized by other members of the white community. This was to be the case until an adequate number of black teachers were available to meet the demand.

The native white in North Carolina had mixed feelings about the white teacher's role in educating black children. In addition to their general opposition to the education of blacks, native whites resented the presence of northern white teachers, the largest single group of teachers working with black children, because they were outsiders. They were thought of as intruders interfering with North Carolina's internal political and social affairs. The comments made by Noble are typical of the attitudes expressed and acted upon by native whites in North Carolina toward the end of the 1860s:

The stranger politicians apparently handled the question of educating the Negro for present political results at the polls rather than for the permanent good of the colored man. The good people in the North too often failed to select discreet persons to administer their generous contributions for the uplift of the freedmen. Many of the northern teachers who were sent into the state came here apparently on the lookout for ostracism as the penalty of their jobs and doggedly seeking it as an evidence of success in their mission, and often purposely stigmatizing their work in the eyes of the native whites by mingling socially with pupils and parents. Of course this does not apply to all who came from the North to establish Negro schools. Many of them were faithful, earnest, and successful teachers who at all times retained their own self-respect and won the good-will and support of the resident white people, as they daily spent their strength in teaching colored children and in training them for useful lives in the state. However, all these unfortunate phases of Negro education were hurting the cause of the colored children, which sooner or later would be taken up by the state when it came into the management of white leaders.[17]

It was Noble's judgment that the education of black youth would best be served when it was under the management of native whites who had the best interests of blacks at heart. However, all evidence up to that time did not support his contention.

The legal establishment of black schools appears to have had its beginnings when a resolution was proposed by the chairman of the committee on education, Jacob W. Bowman, and passed by the house. The resolution was to provide "for the establishment of different public schools for the white and colored races." The vote for passage was ninety-one to two, with the two black members casting the negative votes. It did not take long for former white supporters to bow to the will of a small minority of conservatives. This was the forerunner of a long series of events that led to the complete separation of public schools for blacks and whites—the dual school system.

As far as could be determined, North Carolina was the first state to appoint a black as the assistant superintendent of public instruction, on September 23, 1868: J.W. Hood, the legislator from Cumberland County who had been so concerned all along with providing black children with good education.

This new officer's official duty was the general supervision of the public school interests of the colored children. The office was a creation of the Board of Education and was thought to have been created to satisfy the views of Hood as to the duty of the state to entrust the education of colored children to colored people. He was given, therefore, the specific duty of supervising the public schools of the colored race. Before these schools were established, he devoted his time to visiting and inspecting the colored schools which had been established or aided by the Freedmen's Bureau and the several benevolent organizations which were interested in the education of colored children. His report to Ashley is of historical value because it gives the reader a pretty accurate account of what was being done for North Carolina colored children by their friends just after the war while there were no public schools in operation. At the date of his report, April 22, 1869, the various agencies, not including the Freedmen's Bureau, were maintaining, in whole or in part, 152 schools with 224 teachers, and an enrollment of 11,826 pupils. Hood urged the need of one or more normal schools for the training of colored teachers. Remembering his speech in the constitutional convention on the separation of the races in the schools, it was but natural for him to say with evident reluctance, that "as there appears to be an objection amounting to a prohibition of the use of the unoccupied buildings at Chapel Hill by colored pupils" perhaps the best that can be done is to establish several normal schools in the state at places having "the largest number of good material."[18]

It is evident that there was a serious commitment at the state level to establishing a sound public school system for black children. Unfortunately, efforts at that level were always subject to the actions of local communities. This may explain in part why black public schools developed the way they did from their beginning to the present.

During the formative years of the black school system in North Carolina, the Republican party, with the support of black citizens, controlled state politics. Publicly supported black schools had their birth under this administration in the 1873-74 school year, less than ten years after the end of the Civil War. During their political lifetime the Republicans laid the groundwork for the North Carolina public school system in general and the black school system in particular.

Unquestionably, blacks made phenomenal progress immediately following the Civil War. In 1836, the black population in North Carolina was approximately 36 percent of the total population. Until 1864 no black children were educated in public schools. In fact, during that period it was a misdemeanor to teach black children to read. Even though public schools for blacks were only established in 1873, in the same year approximately 30 percent of salaries paid to teachers were paid to black teachers, 34 percent of the children in the state between the ages of six and twenty-one years were black, 32 percent of the school children were black, 27 percent of the examined and approved teachers were black, and 30 percent of all schools were attended by black students. On a quantitative basis, blacks were almost receiving public school education in proportion to the number of black students available for schooling.

As for wages, the average salaries paid to black teachers, especially black males, in the period 1886-1903 compared fairly well with those paid to white teachers considering the few unskilled positions open to blacks at the time. In 1896 black male teachers made significantly more than their white counterparts, male or female: $1.95 more than white males and $5.06 more than white females. The salaries of black male teachers during the period 1886-1902 exceeded those of white females in five separate years. Black female teachers, however, were consistently paid less than any other group.

It is well to keep in mind that, except for farm workers, no other group of regularly employed persons made less money than teachers.[19] However, since blacks had little choice in type of employment, with most jobs simply closed to them on the basis of race and with those jobs available drastically underpaid, teaching offered not only something approaching a living wage, but high status in the black community as well.

The Twentieth Century

As the nineteenth century drew to a close, the white supremacist movement gathered steam, so that while Charles B. Aycock claimed that "universal" education meant education for all, black and white, others went to work to ensure that "all" meant all whites. In the same election (1900) that brought the Democrats back into power and elected Aycock, a proponent of universal education, governor, an amendment was passed that essentially disfranchised the blacks. The constitutional amendment specified that all voters must be able to read and write. A grandfather clause was included to allay the fears of those counties where white illiteracy was high, stating that until 1908 any adult white illiterate would be permanently registered to vote because his grandfather had voted in 1866, before blacks had gained the vote. The North Carolina Supreme Court ruled in 1902 that black children were entitled to the same per capita share of school funds as whites, but in 1905 it ruled that only "equal facilities must be provided," and it defined equal facilities in 1906: "The school term shall be of the same length during the school year, and that a sufficient number of teachers competent to teach the children in each building or section, shall be employed at such prices as the board may deem proper."[20] And the boards saw fit to pay black teachers an average salary over 30 percent less than whites, about a 20 percent drop in comparison to salaries in the 1890s.[21] Actual facilities provided for black school children also deteriorated at this time.

It is against this backdrop that rural public high schools first came into being in North Carolina. Before 1907 there were three types of high schools in the state: private high schools, subscription schools, and large town and city high schools. The first two types required students to pay, and the third type, available only to those students whose families lived in urban areas, could serve only a minority of students in such a highly rural state.

The general assembly, recognizing the need for high school instruction in rural areas and small towns, passed the 1907 High School Law, which established a fund to stimulate high school instruction in towns of less than 1200 and in rural areas.[22] Needless to say, most of the money went to establishing white rural high schools. By 1915 the expenditures for the white child were 300 percent more than for the black (in 1890 they had been a mere 50 percent more).[23] In 1914 the first three public black high schools were opened, and in 1919 the first black high schools were accredited, four public and seven private. In 1923 the first high schools supported and run by city or county school administrative units received accreditation. In 1923-24, all of ten years after the first black public high schools were opened, there were fourteen public and twenty private accredited black high schools. These accredited schools served 87 percent of the black students enrolled in high school at the time. Ten years later, 1933-34, there were 106 public and ten private accredited black high schools serving almost 98 percent of blacks enrolled in high school.[24]

These figures do not reflect, of course, the number of children who never even got to high school. Among whites it was estimated in 1924 that there were more than 50,000 rural children who ought to have been in high school but were not. In that year there were only 332 standard accredited high schools in the state, and more than thirty counties had no such standard high school. The *Report of the Superintendent of Public Instruction* states that there were more than six hundred high schools in the state. This would include black and white public and private accredited and nonaccredited schools.[25] Of the 332 accredited public high schools, only fourteen, or 4.2 percent, were black.[26] The approximately 50,000 white rural children who were not receiving high school instruction represented over 40 percent of high school age white children.[27] Blacks who attended public high school represented 4.6 percent of the total enrollment of students in such high schools.[28] We have found no estimates of how many black children of high school age were not receiving high school instruction, but it must have been extremely high during this period.

During the 1920s, along with the growth in numbers of black high schools, blacks once again gained some control, at the state level, over their education. No black had been in such a position since J.W. Hood was appointed assistant superintendent of public instruction in 1868. In 1921 the North Carolina general assembly authorized the establishment of a Division of Negro Education in the State Department of Public Instruction.[29] This division was to have a director and such supervisors and assistants as were necessary to complete its designated assignment. Its specific duties were to monitor all the black normal, training, elementary, and high schools and teacher-training departments.

By 1933-34, even with 106 public black high schools in operation, in seventy-one counties with black school populations of 1000 or more, there were seventeen county and five city administrative units with no black high schools and an additional thirteen county and four city administrative units that did not support their accredited black high schools. Thirty-three of these counties, with a total of forty-eight accredited black high schools, had facilities inadequate for both the size and population of the county. Of the remaining twenty-nine counties with black school populations of less than 1000, sixteen had no high school facilities for blacks, six counties provided less than four years of high school instruction; only four counties had an accredited four-year black high school, and one county had a four-year unaccredited black high school.[30] These figures come from a study made by a commission appointed by Governor J.C.B. Ehringhaus, half of whose members were black. The report of the commission, published at the request of the governor, recommended:

1. that small schools be consolidated into modern school plants and that adequate transportation be provided;
2. needed rooms be added to existing schools and schools built where there were none or where they were inadequate;
3. black teachers be able to receive adequate teacher training at the post-high-school level;
4. that black schools operate for a term of not less than eight months;
5. that the black high school curriculum include vocational training and that black teachers receive training in the area of guidance; and
6. that black teachers receive "equal pay for equal training and equal service" and that the differential between black teachers' salaries and those of white teachers be reduced by 50 percent in 1935 and eliminated totally within three to five years after that.[31]

A major impetus to providing public high school education for both blacks and whites during the 1930s was almost certainly linked to the economic conditions. With the high rate of adult unemployment, the last thing the state wanted was an additional influx of adolescents each year on the job market. Parents also became aware that the better trained worker had a better chance of being employed.[32]

Although equalizing the salaries of black and white teachers was one of the major recommendations of the governor's commission, it was not until almost ten years later, that the general assembly voluntarily passed a law requiring that the salaries be equalized. This made North Carolina the first among the southern states to take such action. The educational level of black teachers, which in 1924-25 stood at about four years of high school, in 1933-34 averaged about two years of college; for whites the figures were a year and a half and three and three-quarter years of college.[33] As the country became involved in World War II, white teachers found more profitable jobs in areas other than teaching. This did not hold true for black teachers. As a result of this, white teachers left their professions in great numbers, and by 1948 there were sixty times more nonstandard certificate holders among white teachers than in 1937.[34]

Thus, by 1947-48 the quality of teacher training and preparation for blacks and whites was reversed from what it had been in 1924-25. In fact, from 1941 to 1948, the number of white teachers teaching on nonstandard certificates rose from 1022 to 2909, while the number of black teachers holding "A" (standard) certificates went from 5806 to 6240.[35] Whatever the reason for this shift, black children certainly benefited. The general feeling about this shift in quality was that "disaster threatens the white schools."[36] But if the quality of teaching was a bright spot in black education, all was not rosy. The 1948 *Report of the State Education Commission* stated:

The Negro schools deserve special consideration. Generally speaking, they are in much worse condition than the white schools. In 1945 over 60 percent of the Negro high school children of the state were enrolled in schools below the standard required for accreditment. Of the 201 Negro high schools, 96 employed from one to three teachers. Children attending these schools cannot receive credits required for entrance to college.[37]

Two court decisions in the late thirties and many decisions throughout the forties began to undermine the "separate but equal" policies at the graduate and professional school level. In what must have been an effort to prevent further challenge to the doctrine of "separate but equal," the entire South began to spend an unprecedented proportion of its income for the education of Negro children in public schools.[38] By the early 1950s, North Carolina was spending significantly more per pupil on black children than it had in 1940. In 1940, $41.69 was spent per white child and $27.30 per black child. The amount spent on each black child was 65 percent of that spent on each white child. By the 1950-51 school year $152.20 was spent per white child and $128.67 per black child. This last figure was 85 percent of the amount spent on each white child.[39] In this ten-year period North Carolina increased by 20 percent the comparative amounts it spent on each of its black school children.

Continuing the trend that had begun in the late thirties and which had caused so much concern over the quality of instruction in the white schools, black teacher preparation continued to improve, until by 1949-50 it surpassed that of white teachers. The white teacher spent an average of 3.8 years in college in 1949-50, while the black teacher spent 4.0, and in 1950-51 the figures were 3.9 for whites and 4.1 for blacks.[40] Salaries also reflected this difference in training, since the law passed in 1944 equalized salary schedules. Black teachers salaries were 103 percent those of white teachers in 1950-51 as opposed to 73 percent of whites' salaries in 1940.

Compared with most of the other southern states, North Carolina was making good headway in equalizing educational opportunities for black school children. However, on May 17, 1954 the decision destined to change the face of southern education was handed down by the Supreme Court. The opinion, which was unanimous, read in part: "We conclude that in the field of public education the doctrine of 'separate but equal' has no place. Separate educational facilities are inherently unequal."[41]

In 1957-58 three large cities in North Carolina—Charlotte, Greensboro, and Winston-Salem—put into effect a desegregation plan based on pupil placement, making them among the first communities in the Deep South to take such action. However, the plan had limited effects on the actual makeup of most student bodies in the area, since parents actually had to request that their children be placed in other schools. As might be expected, the only whites requesting transfers were those into whose school the few blacks asked to transfer.[42]

It would be a mistake to imply that after that things went smoothly. They did not. North Carolina was one of the six southern states in 1960 that passed private school laws with tuition grants establishing so-called "free" private schools. North Carolina also still maintained pupil-placement laws and, in fact, was one of ten southern states to vote school-closing laws.[43] This was part of the political reality. But what must be remembered is that of all the states in the South, North Carolina in this century has shown the most concern for its black school children and has spent more on them comparatively speaking than any of the other states.[44] The thrust during the fifties was to equalize educational facilities and opportunities for black children. No matter what the reasons, the black children benefited. And whatever one may feel about the rationale for the attempts to close the educational gap between black and white, it still remains that other southern states did not make the effort, did not care enough to spend the extra money. Now we can turn our attention to our present concern: The effects of black high schools on community development in North Carolina.

4   The Black High School

While a comprehensive statistical summary was compiled from records of the North Carolina State Department of Education (Appendix B), in order to gain a broader picture of the black high school in 1963-64, data were also obtained from other sources.

Background on the Black High School

In the spring of 1973, letters were sent to the superintendents of 151 school districts asking them to give the names of the all black high schools that had been operating in their districts in 1963-64, the name of the principal of each school in 1963-64, and the last year each of these schools had functioned as an all-black high school. One hundred and eight responses were received, providing a list of 177 formerly all-black high schools.

Questionnaires were then mailed to the seventy-six principals for whom we had current addresses. Names of other principals were obtained from the 1963-64 Educational Directory of North Carolina and questionnaires were sent to them at their last known address. In total, 187 questionnaires were sent out, and forty-one were returned. Cards were then mailed to remind the principals to return the questionnaire, resulting in the receipt of seventeen more questionnaires. Two were received too late for processing. The combined mailings resulted in the receipt of fifty-eight questionnaires, which were processed in the fall of 1973.

The High School Setting

Most of the principals (40 percent) answering the questionnaire administered schools located in the eastern part of North Carolina. About 59 percent of these black high schools were in rural areas or in small towns of less than two thousand. The majority (60 percent) of the students in the black high schools represented came from rural areas.

Only 3 percent of the principals reported a black population of less than 10 percent of the total in the community in which the school was located. Fifty-three percent of the principals reported that the black population was 10 to 50 percent of the total.

35

Sixteen percent of the principals reported that they had twenty or fewer teachers on their staff. The largest percentage (64 percent) indicated that they had from twenty-one to forty teachers on their staff. Ninety percent of the principals reported that 75 to 100 percent of their teachers held masters degrees. Only 2 percent of the principals reported that less than 10 percent of their teachers held an "A" certificate. The student teacher ratio in the black high schools ranged from less than 20:1 to more than 35:1. Only 28 percent of the principals reported a student-teacher ratio of less than 25:1, while 65 percent of them reported a student-teacher ratio of 25:1 or greater.

Seventy-five percent of the principals reported that their schools were fully accredited, while only 10 percent reported that their schools were not accredited. Ninety-seven percent of the principals reported that their schools had ceased to operate as all-black schools by 1972. Only 7 percent of the principals reported that their formerly all-black schools contained grades nine through twelve after desegregation.

The High School Students

Of the principals responding, 38 percent reported that 10 to 25 percent of the students came from one-parent homes, while only 4 percent reported that 50 to 100 percent of the students came from one-parent homes. The majority of principals (59 percent) indicated that 50 to 100 percent of the students came from homes in which the parents were churchgoers. With respect to the marriage age of black youth, 52 percent of the principals reported that males married between the ages of nineteen and twenty-one, while 62 percent reported the females married at this age. By the time they were twenty-one, 55 percent of the males and 76 percent of the females were married. Almost half of the principals (45 percent) reported that 10 to 25 percent of their students dropped out before completing the twelfth grade, while one-fourth reported a dropout rate of less than 10 percent, and one-fourth reported a dropout rate of 25 to 50 percent. Almost half of the principals (48 percent) reported that less than 10 percent of the students worked part time while attending high school. Only 3 percent of the principals indicated that over half of their graduating seniors went on to college or technical training schools. Approximately half of the principals (52 percent) indicated that 10 to 25 percent of the students went on to college, and almost half of the principals (41 percent) indicated that 10 to 25 percent of the students went on to technical training schools. One-fourth of the principals (24 percent) reported that less than 10 percent of their students remained in the community after graduation, while approximately half (52 percent) reported that 10 to 50 percent of the students remained in the community.

Of the principals reporting, 45 percent felt that approximately 50 to 75 percent of the parents were interested in their children obtaining good grades.

Forty percent of the principals reported that 25 to 50 percent of the parents were interested in their children's involvement in extracurricular activities, while 45 percent reported that 25 to 50 percent were interested in the activities of the school. A smaller percentage, 10 to 25 percent of the parents, were reported by 45 percent of the principals to be actively interested in other community organizations. Over half of the principals (55 percent) reported that the parents were not very well informed concerning local and regional political events, while 34 percent felt that they were fairly well informed.

Program Structure of the Black
High School

When black high school principals were asked about the curriculum departments that comprised their schools, their responses varied. Table 4-1 shows the percentage of principals who reported the existence of the various curriculum departments in their schools.

Student Enrollment

Nine percent of the principals reported that they had a total enrollment of fewer than five hundred students in their school; 29 percent of the principals indicated that they had from 500-799 students, 25 percent of them said that they had from 800-899 students, and the remaining 37 percent of the principals reported

Table 4-1
Subject Matter Departments in Black High Schools

Curriculum Departments in Schools	Percent of Principals Responding Yes
1 Mathematics	97
2 Social Studies	97
3 English	95
4 Home Economics	93
5 Science	93
6 Foreign Language	84
7 Business Training	84
8 Music	81
9 Industrial Arts	71
10 Technical Training	28
11 Art	26
12 Any Others	28

that they had more than 1000 students in their schools. Only 7 percent of the principals reported that they had more than 1500 students in their schools.

Eleven percent of the principals reported a high school enrollment of less than 200; 34 percent of the principals reported a high school enrollment from 200-399 students, 29 percent reported a high school enrollment from 400-599 students, and 14 percent reported a high school enrollment from 600-799 students. Only 12 percent of the principals reported high school enrollments of 800 or more students.

Twenty-one percent of the principals reported that their schools graduated fewer than forty students in the last graduating class prior to desegregation, 32 percent reported a graduating class of from 40-79 students, 24 percent reported a graduating class of from 80-119 students, and 15 percent reported a graduating class of more than 120 students.

Number of Teachers in High School

Thirty-one percent of the principals indicated that they had ten or fewer teachers in grades 9-12, 29 percent reported from 11 to 20 teachers at that level, 21 percent reported from 21 to 30 teachers, and 12 percent had from 31 to 40 teachers. Only 5 percent of the principals reported having a teaching staff of 41 or more teachers at the high school level.

Extracurricular Activities

Thirty-six percent of the principals reported that more than half of their student body participated in extracurricular activities. The largest percentage of principals responding (38 percent) placed the percentage of students participating as somewhere between 25 and 50 percent. Principals generally believed that there was a high positive correlation when athletic achievement and extracurricular leadership are correlated with scholastic achievement.

A large percentage of black principals indicated that their interscholastic teams belonged to regional conferences. The largest percentage (86 percent) of principals reported that their basketball teams belonged to regional conferences. Similarly, in regard to interscholastic teams competing for the state championship, the majority of principals (78 percent) reported that their basketball teams had participated in state championship play. A number of schools participated in statewide competition in nonathletic extracurricular activities. The largest percentage of principals reported that their chorus participated in state-wide activities (47 percent) and contests (50 percent). Forty-three percent of the principals reported that their bands participated in state-wide activities and contests. Thirty-four percent of the principals reported that the drama club participated in statewide activities, while 36 percent reported their drama clubs' involvement in statewide contests.

Support for Extracurricular Activities. A large majority of principals (80 percent) rated the school spirit at their schools as quite high to very high. Almost half of the principals (48 percent) reported that parental involvement in school activities was moderate. Community support for and interest in the schools' athletic teams was rated as strong or very strong by 66 percent of the principals.

The two major sources of financial support for extracurricular activities were concessions on the school premises (26 percent) and community fund-raising drives (38 percent). Finally, when black principals were asked how often school facilities were used for community related meetings and organizations, 45 percent indicated that they were used often to very often. It is almost impossible, however, to quantify this measure since "often" and "very often" meant different things in different places.

The extensiveness of the black high school's extracurricular activity program was more or less dependent on geographic location (city or rural) and size (large or small). Basic to most high schools was some kind of athletic program, usually basketball and/or football. Those activities in which many students participated across the state included band, vocal music, drama, and student council. Debating was also a statewide activity but did not sustain the interest of all schools. In addition, students were involved in a number of other activities such as majorettes, cheerleaders, yearbook, school newspaper, service clubs, and content clubs at many schools. The black high school's extracurricular activity program seems to have reached its peak in the late 1950s and early 1960s. Generally, those activities that were spasmodic in terms of interest and degree of participation and were locally sponsored (not involved in any competition between schools) were less likely to make strong and lasting impressions on most people asked to describe how that particular activity functioned in their school in 1963-64.

Major Extracurricular Activities. The major extracurricular activities of the black high school, with descriptions of their function, membership, and means of financial support provide a composite picture of the environmental setting of the average school's program.

Band. Questionnaires were filled out by eleven band directors of formerly all-black high schools; ten directors had bachelor's degrees in instrumental music and three had master's degrees in music education. All the band directors indicated that their schools had had concert and marching bands, eight also had pep bands, five had jazz bands as well, and three had other organizations such as woodwind and brass ensembles, symphonic band, or beginners band. Membership in the concert band ranged from forty to eight-five students, in the marching band from fifty to 125 students, while in the other band organizations, it averaged about twenty-five students. In most schools the concert and marching bands rehearsed daily; other groups had either no scheduled rehearsals or met one to five times weekly. The band directors reported that their concert bands performed from three to sixteen times annually, with six performances as the average, while the marching band performed twelve to twenty-two times a year. The other organizations had from one to twenty-two performances a year, with groups such as the pep band, which played at athletic events, performing ɯe most often.

According to the band directors, all their students had previous band experience in the junior high school; five reported that students had also taken part in an elementary school instrumental music program, and one said that his students had previously taken private lessons. In general, there was little opportunity for the students to study privately in high school unless lessons were provided by the band director.

All the band directors indicated that some of the money for the bands' expenses was provided by fund-raising drives carried on by students and the community. Five directors cited the school budget as the source for some of the funds, particularly for music and instruments. Money for band uniforms was often obtained through fund-raising activities, but in all cases except one, in which the Band Parents owned the uniforms, the uniforms were donated to the school. All the schools owned at least some of the instruments, usually the larger ones. At some schools students paid rental fees to use the instruments while other schools lent them free of charge. The band directors reported that from 10 to 90 percent of the students owned their own instruments.

All but one director said that the bands participated in state and local band contests; one school's marching band competed at the Cherry Blossom Parade in Washington, D.C. All the band directors indicated that majorettes were associated with the band, and many had baton twirlers, flag bearers, and letter girls as well.

As a part of the black public school band program, district and state band festivals were held annually. They were sponsored by the North Carolina Band and Orchestra Directors Associations. All school bands were eligible for participation if they met the conditions outlined in "Rules Governing the State and District Festivals." The rules in question are the following:

1. All schools must participate in district festivals before they are eligible for admission to the state festival.
2. Organization and soloist must compete in the same class in the state festival in which they compete in the district festival.
3. All soloists will perform from memory.
4. A copy of all music must be furnished to the judges in both district and state

festivals. Music so furnished will be returned to the owners following the festival.

5. Individuals or groups planning to perform "for criticism only" must give three weeks notice to the district and state chairman. Groups or individuals who plan to attend the state festival on this basis must participate in the district festival.

Each school performed in the class to which it was assigned on the basis of school size and diversity of the band and music experiences provided. Individuals and groups from each school were expected to compete within the class to which they were assigned. The range and quality of the music used by bands for performing in festivals covered many types of music, from Mozart and Wagner to "Whistle While You Work."

Choral Groups. In choir, students often received instruction in sight-reading and they performed a wide range of music. The range of music types included classical, folk, popular, and tunes from musicals. The selection of music was geared to give students a broad and well-rounded exposure to many types of music reflecting the experiences and feelings of different kinds of people in a variety of settings. When choir was a part of the curriculum, classes in boys' and girls' chorus as well as in mixed chorus were held daily. Evening and afternoon rehearsals were held when preparing for performances such as concerts and festivals. Many groups participated annually in their district festival and could advance to the state festival if they received top ratings. In general, the choral groups were open to any interested student. At an average-sized school, about eighty to ninety students participated in the program with forty to sixty students in the top performing group. Financial support for the choral groups was obtained through the school's miscellaneous fund and through individual assessments made by the principal of students and/or faculty.

Student Council. The student council served as the governing body of the school from the students' standpoint. In general, it provided (1) a forum for students, (2) an opportunity for students to develop leadership ability and learn parliamentary procedures, (3) an opportunity for students to learn through self-direction, (4) a bridge between the students and the administration and faculty, (5) activities and projects for students, and (6) activities designed to foster good public relations. The student council at most schools was affiliated with the North Carolina Association of Student Councils, an all-black group, and the National Association of Student Councils, which was composed of high schools throughout the country regardless of the racial make-up of the school. Each summer, leadership workshops were sponsored by the State Association. The student council usually met once a week after school with 85 to 100 percent attendance. The council was composed of one representative elected from each homeroom class, and the president was elected by the entire student body. Financial support for the council was often obtained through a voluntary student council fee, and through profits from concession stands at athletic events.

Debate. The debate club provided the opportunity for students to build confidence and improve voice control, diction, and stage decorum. The students competed with other members of the club, and many schools competed in state and local debate contests. The group was open to any interested student; membership averaged from twenty-five to thirty members yearly. Financial support generally came from school miscellaneous funds.

Dramatics. Most drama groups were affiliated with the North Carolina High School Drama Association. The ultimate aim of the group was to provide varied experiences in acting, staging, and costuming. In general, two to five hours after school daily and five to seven hours on weekends, over about an eight-week period, were required to prepare for a production. Many groups participated in annual district drama festivals. The drama group was open to any interested student; often as many as sixty or seventy students were members. Once he participated in the activities of the group, a student had the opportunity to be inducted into the National Thespian Society, an honorary group, based on points earned by performing in and working on the productions. Financial support for the drama group came mainly from ticket sales.

New Farmers of America (NFA). NFA was an organization for boys aged fifteen and above studying vocational agriculture; it was designed to assist them in the development of leadership and other related abilities, and was closely related to their classroom work. The group met twice a month during the school day and often daily for one hour after school; when preparing for contests three to six hours of meetings a week were often required. The groups competed annually in parliamentary procedure, tool identification, public speaking, quartet singing, livestock and soil judging, and forestry contests. Membership included those enrolled in vocational agriculture classes and usually averaged about eighty students. Financial support came from dues and fund-raising projects.

New Homemakers of America (NHA). NHA was an organization for girls enrolled or formerly enrolled in home economics courses, and was designed to provide meaningful experiences for students through various activities such as preparing for an annual mother-daughter banquet. Membership in the group averaged about fifty students, and financial support came from dues and special fund-raising projects.

4-H Club. The 4-H Club, no longer run by the school as of 1960, was actually a county-wide organization open to youth aged nine to nineteen. The club was designed to provide economic, social, physical, and spiritual experience for the students through individual and group projects. County, district, and state competition in areas such as clothing and livestock, as well as dress reviews, public speaking, and talent shows were sponsored by the 4-H organization. Approximately one hundred project areas and thirty activities were available for students. More girls than boys were usually involved, and more students participated in rural areas than in urban areas. Financial support was provided through the Agricultural Extension Agency.

National Honor Society. The National Honor Society, an organization composed of students whose average was "B" or higher, functioned as a service group which helped teachers, students, and the community. Membership was open to students in the eleventh and twelfth grades, and generally included 5 to 10 percent of the school. Financial support was obtained through membership dues and special projects.

Library Club. The library club was a service group which aided the librarian in issuing and checking in books, taking inventory, and preparing new acquisitions for shelving. Any student could join; membership averaged from seven to twelve members. Many library clubs were affiliated with the North Carolina Student Library Association, and money was raised through dues.

Cheerleaders. Cheerleaders were often an important adjunct to the high school athletic program, functioning to keep school spirit high at basketball and football games. Membership was determined by tryout, with the selection being made by an advisor or a faculty committee. Financial support for the group came from school funds and individual assessments.

Yearbook. Student involvement in producing a school yearbook varied greatly from school to school. Working on the yearbook gave students an opportunity to gain experience in the various facets of producing such a book, from soliciting ads to writing copy and preparing layouts. In general, only members of the senior class were involved in the production of the yearbook. Financial support was obtained through the sales of ads and through student fees.

Content Clubs. Many schools had organizations of students with similar interests in an academic area for the purpose of providing enriching experiences and expanding on classroom work through related activities and projects. Most of these clubs were organized as French clubs, and sometimes as math and science clubs. Membership was open to any student with a strong interest in the area, and generally ranged from ten to twenty members. Any financial support required by the group was obtained through fund-raising projects.

Majorettes. Majorettes were expected to perform both with the marching band and alone as a unit. Training classes were often held for three to four weeks in the summer prior to selection. Practices were held after school daily, and many hours were spent preparing for special performances if the group participated in state clinics. The group usually consisted of ten to thirteen girls selected by a judging board, and it was often required that they be members of the band. Financial support for the group came mainly from individual assessments and group projects.

School Newspaper. While many schools had newspapers, some were published as often as once a week and some as seldom as twice a year. The involvement of students in this activity was dependent, then, on the size of the newspaper and its frequency of publication. Any student was allowed to work on the paper, although English students and typing students were most often involved. Money was obtained through the sale of ads, through student fees, and through the sale of the paper itself.

The All-Black High School as Viewed by Individuals

The views of superintendents, teachers and special staff, parents and students, and leaders of the black community provided a different perspective on the formerly all black high school. In general, the comments of all these individuals centered on the roles they had played in the all-black high schools, the advantages and disadvantages of the dual school system, and the effects of the loss of the black high school.

Superintendents

In discussing the black high school, all the superintendents commented on the role of the black school in the community, its financial problems, and how the black school compared with the white school in facilities, programs and faculty.

In the 1930s the state government took over the responsibility for funding the operation of the public schools. This meant that approximately 70 percent of each school district's budget came from the state, with the rest provided by local funds. While black and white schools were thus made somewhat equal by state policy, differences existed in regard to such things as teachers' salary supplements and coaches' supplements, both paid for out of local funds. For example, in 1963-64 the black basketball coach in one town earned a $300 supplement, while the white coach earned $1800. Since money from the state was to be used for the operation of the schools and not for capital improvements, it was up to the local school districts to provide funds for new buildings and for remodeling old ones. The effects of this policy differed from district to district, but in general it resulted in inferior facilities for black schools. This was owing, in part, to pressure by the white power structure at the local level on the central administration to spend most of the local funds on white schools, and, in part, to the inability of many poor, predominantly black districts to raise much money through taxation at the local level. One other policy that put the black high school at a disadvantage was basing the allotment of money on average daily attendance. This meant that a white school with 95 percent attendance could basically get the money in the state budget to which it was entitled, while a black school, which during certain seasons of the year might have had attendance as low as 50 percent, would lose teachers as well as funds for student supplies.

Because of this shortage of funds, the black principal was forced to find money elsewhere for school improvements, supplies, athletic programs, and possibly even teachers' salaries. Much of this money came from Booster Clubs, PTA fund-raising drives, and "benevolent" funds to which individuals in the community were asked to contribute. Most of the superintendents did not seem to know much about these hidden budgets, but they were apparently tolerated because they were essential to the operation of the black high school.

Black schools were often described as "tight ships" run under authoritarian rule. While "this autocratic, dictatorial way of doing things gets speedier results than anything else, this tight ship was used to keep the school in order rather than to effect curriculum improvement." One superintendent went on to say that it was probably true that the black schools enforced their rules very stringently, but he suggested that the rules they set differed somewhat from the rules set in the white schools. Rules dealing with tardiness and truancy, for instance, were not enforced.

They were handicapped with the lack of attendance. It's awfully hard to enforce attendance rules when you really have little control over it. They tried to control it; they'd even go around and find out why the children were working when they should be in school, but they were limited in that they'd get reprisals if they tried to enforce certain regulations. They couldn't set a rule that if you damage or lose something you're going to have to pay for it, because in some cases there may not be resources to collect. They were masters at knowing what rules were enforceable and what rules they couldn't enforce. They couldn't enforce things like attendance and tardiness, so they didn't set rules regarding these things. . . . In other words, they set rules that were reasonable to that group of students.

Most of the superintendents viewed the black school as weak and inferior. Several believed that black teachers, although well qualified on paper, were in reality not as well qualified as white teachers. The athletic program was described by one superintendent as good, but as not in the same league with those in the white schools. The calibre of the players was high, but they had fewer coaches, less equipment, less time, and also a different attitude toward sports. "They played football because they enjoyed playing football, and they normally played it well as individuals, but they did not, in my opinion, ever get the discipline necessary to form a team."

Several of the superintendents felt that the high schools did not meet the needs of the students, particularly in regard to course offerings. The dropout rate, described by one superintendent as about 50 percent from the eighth grade enrollment to graduating seniors, "might seem to indicate that we were not meeting the needs of all the students." Another superintendent suggested that the problem in his district, where the curriculum hadn't changed since 1933, applied to the whites as well as the blacks. None of the students in his district had been able to get any vocational training in school beyond what was offered in the standard home economics and agricultural courses. Recognition of this need led eventually to the establishment of a technical high school in this district with courses such as masonry, health occupations, carpentry, and commercial cooking.

Despite its academic shortcomings, the black high school played an important role as the focal point of the black community. It served as the rallying point and meeting place for political and social community affairs. In many small towns the school was the only place where two hundred or three hundred people could gather for a dance or meeting. There was much more participation from the black community than from the white in activities dealing with the high school. This might be attributed to the fact that there were fewer outside activities available to blacks than there were for whites at that stage. The school provided more opportunities for the black people to come together. In other words, a PTA meeting became a major social event that blacks looked forward to attending.

The advent of integration was viewed by the superintendents as having both advantages and disadvantages. Desegregation not only destroyed the black/white dichotomy, but it also destroyed the poor white school and the influence of the school. The chief advantage of integration was generally agreed to be this equalization of facilities, instruction, and funds. The school consolidations that usually accompanied integration were partly responsible for the improved quality of programs and instruction, since larger schools could attract better staff and provide more resources.

On the negative side, both black and white students probably felt that they lost the school that used to belong to them. Another disadvantage of the integrated system is the fact that many black students lost opportunities for leadership roles that they had had under the segregated system. One of the superintendents pointed out that the problem here is not a problem of desegregation but rather one of consolidation. "You've reduced the number of schools and if you do that you're going to reduce the number of leadership roles."

The school also no longer could be used for social functions by either white or black groups. Black parents and the black community as a whole could no longer identify with the integrated school, and they turned away from it. Unfortunately, nothing has come along to replace the black school as the central unifying force in the black community.

Teachers and Special Staff

Nine teachers and special staff members were interviewed, five men and four women ranging in age from thirty-two to fifty-three. All had been born in the South, were black, and had at least a bachelor's degree. These nine were selected because they had been coaches, band directors, music teachers, or directors of other extracurricular activities in the school. All described the student participation in these activities as excellent. The organizations were ones that the black community identified with proudly. Boosters' Clubs and the PTA worked actively to raise money to support these extracurricular activities. The school was the cultural center of the community, and with the exception of the church, all that was happening for youth and adults centered around school programs.

Despite the advantages of integration, such as better facilities and more funds, many of these teachers saw integration as being more to the students' disadvantage. "The all-black school afforded a haven for the black students and a community-center for the black parents. The average and below average black students have no ties or feelings of belonging to the now integrated school." Fewer black students now participate in activities, partly because they do not identify with the school, and partly, some of these teachers feel, because they are not encouraged to participate as they were in the past. The black students are now "segregated in an integrated school." Lack of student involvement means, of course, that the parents no longer have an opportunity to assist their children or to express themselves through school-related activities, as they once did.

Parents

Twenty-six parents were interviewed, ranging in age from thirty-five to sixty-five. All but four were born in North Carolina, and those four were born elsewhere in the South. Thirteen of the parents had been raised on farms, three in small towns, and eight in moderate-sized cities. They ranged in educational background from many parents with an elementary school education to one parent with a bachelor's degree and two with master's degrees. In terms of income, twelve earned less than $5000 a year, seven earned $5000 to $6999, and the highest income was in the $12,000 to $12,999 bracket. Most of the parents had children who had graduated from all-black schools, and some had children who had graduated from integrated schools.

When questioned about their participation as parents in the extracurricular activities of the school, all but three said they had been involved in activities such as PTA, Band Boosters, Band Mothers, and other fund-raising activities. Most of these parents also participated in other community organizations unrelated to the school.

In talking about the advantages and disadvantages of integration, parents were not in agreement about whether or not their children were getting a better education under the integrated system. Many felt that the school facilities were better now, that there was more money for instructional supplies, and that the curriculum was better. These advantages were offset by several disadvantages they saw as resulting from integration. Several parents suggested that the segregated school had been located closer to the students' homes. All-black schools gave the students a sense of solidarity. They had been proud of their schools and their accomplishments then, but now they had lost interest in many of the activities, since they no longer identified with the school. Communication among parents, teachers, and students was not as open as it had been under the segregated system. Perhaps most important to the parents was the loss of the school as the center of the community. As one parent said: "Activities there were not just school activities but they were for the whole community, and we looked forward to them." Another said: "We miss the Glee Club, the Better Speech Club, all the plays we had." Another parent added: "We no longer have the opportunity to use effectively some of the talents we were so proud of." In short, the loss of black schools has meant abolishing the school-related activities for parents rather than consolidating them. In addition, parents no longer feel a part of the decision-making process of the school.

Students

Questionnaires were sent to thirty students who had graduated from high schools between 1962 and 1973. Of these, twenty-four had graduated from all-black high schools and six from integrated high schools, although these six had attended all-black high schools previously. Most of the students had been active in at least one extracurricular activity in high school; many had participated in several. Generally, they believed that participation in these activities contributed to their education, taught them to interact with others, and was one of the most enjoyable aspects of their high school experience. Some of the students felt that in the black high school they had better communication with the teachers and more opportunity to participate in extracurricular activities. While the integrated high school provided better facilities and more funds, it also deprived the black students of their sense of identification with the school and gave them a feeling of alienation, leading to decreased participation in activities. Many of the students recognized that their own lack of involvement in activities was accompanied by the withdrawal of their parents and the black community as a whole from the activities of the school. Most students felt that as a result of integration, the school lost its position as the focal point of the black community.

Community Leaders

Eighteen community leaders, including black ministers, local politicians and city council members, were interviewed to determine how they viewed the role of the school in the community, the results of integration, and the advantages and disadvantages of the dual school system.

Most of those interviewed felt that prior to integration the black school served as a rallying point, a social center, and an institution with which the black community could identify. The black school had a close relationship with organizations within the community and sponsoring groups by providing a place for them to meet, while these groups, in turn, often worked to raise money for the school and participated in other general support activities.

The loss of the black school has meant several things to the black community. The public does not feel as close to the schools, and school pride and loyalty have diminished. There is no longer a central meeting place for the black community, or a unifying force that ties the community together as the black school did.

The community leaders felt that generally inter- and intra-community relations have changed very little. As one individual stated: "Relationships between persons cannot be enhanced as long as boundary lines such as race, economics, social and religious factors cause communities to be developed and maintained as clearly defined black and white communities."

Under the dual school system, the people had more pride in their school and their community. Black students were known by their teachers and the administration and were encouraged to develop their capabilities. In the all-black school there were more opportunities to participate in school activities, thus giving these students more leadership experience. The curriculum and facilities of the all-black school were limited, however. Under the dual school system, public funds did not seem to be distributed fairly between black schools and white schools, and blacks were not involved in making policies that affected them.

5   The Black High School Principal

The black high school principal played a number of roles that were outside the terms of his contract and specific training and were not of his choosing. In addition to his legal school and educational responsibilities, the black principal was expected to avoid antagonizing the white community and its power structure while providing services that facilitated the progress and interests of the black community. If he violated the expectations of the former, he would be unceremoniously removed and "blackballed" as an educator, and if he violated the expectations of the latter, he would be ostracized and despised by those whom he served. In effect, the black high school principal was always the man in the middle, expected to deliver something to his various publics who were in basic conflict over the products desired. The black principal was in a "no-win" game that required a winning strategy if he were to justify his efforts as a professional educator, man, and citizen.

Interviews with Former Principals

Perhaps the most striking thing revealed by the men who were formerly principals of all-black high schools was the degree of autonomy they were allowed. This is true of rural schools, such as Fuquay Springs Consolidated, and also of black high schools in urban areas, such as Chapel Hill. Time and again these principals pointed out that so long as things appeared to be running smoothly and the minimum requirements of the law were met, they were left alone. The operative word here is "appeared." One superintendent said to a black principal: "I don't know if you're ugly enough to keep order, but you're big enough." The principals concluded that it really did not matter what was being taught in the schools; the major aim of the black principals' role as it appeared to whites was to keep black children in line, to keep them in their place. This is what many of the principals said about their jobs in black high schools. They didn't all see it necessarily as a negative "keep them in their place" role. They believed it was their responsibility to maintain discipline in their schools. Often this demonstrated ability led troubled school districts in the early years of integration to call back many of these black principals to posts from which they had been unceremoniously dumped a year or two before, to restore order.

Black principals saw maintaining discipline as only a part of their roles. They were most concerned with providing black youngsters with a decent education. Since the white-run central office did not particularly care about this aspect of black schooling, it was in large part left up to the ingenuity of the black principal. And he usually needed a good deal of it too, since adequate funding was rarely forthcoming. Often this was because allocations for per pupil expenditure were made on the basis of attendance figures taken in the early fall, right in the middle of the harvest. Many black children were needed at home during this time. Consequently, even if allocations were made fairly, with all other things being equal, the total amount of money received per pupil by black high schools came to a smaller percentage figured against the total enrollment than was justified by attendance during the school year, excluding the early fall. And, of course, many black schools, which were at the mercy of the central office, did not receive even the share of funds to which they were entitled.

With this as their reality, black principals were faced with the task of providing sufficient supplies, adequate lunch programs, habitable buildings, functioning athletic programs, and various extracurricular activities. It might be said that successful black high-school programs ran on one-third good will, one-third hard work, one-third funds.

Even though the black teachers were often better trained or more highly certified than whites, when they attempted to develop and implement up-to-date programs of instruction they had to cope with hand-me-down texts from the white schools as well as a far lower level of educational achievement and educational experiences in the homes of most black children. Often black parents had completed school only to the fourth grade. They had no books or magazines around, and they frequently didn't see what good further education would do their children in terms of providing greater economic opportunities. Working with this attitude from the home, black principals and teachers had to supply the motivation and the prodding. One principal commented that getting eleventh-graders to read at a nineth-grade level was more of an achievement than was realized, since for so many students printed material was simply not an ordinary part of their home environment.

Just getting the children to school was a problem. Many children lived too far away to make walking to school possible, and in rural areas there was no public transportation. One principal remembered raising money in the late twenties and early thirties to buy a school bus, maintain it, and pay its driver. When the state finally began providing buses in the mid-thirties, the new buses went to the whites and the old ones went to the blacks.

Principals were faced with the problem of providing some kind of lunch program for their schools. Many children would not have eaten had food not been provided. Even before the relationship between protein-poor diet and poor learning abilities was discovered, providing lunches so that children would not go hungry was an important part of a principal's job.

t lunch room program and we'd go out and beg for collard
ke that . . . and old yellow grits . . . to make a lunch for those
ve anything, and those who could pay, paid, and those who
ney we said, "Find some way to feed that child."

cooked and served by two women who gave their services for little
ney. "We felt just as proud having a lunch room under the basement of
a church as they feel now having more."

Another principal said that before his school had a lunch room, teachers and
some of the older girls would cook hot soup on the potbellied stoves that were
in each classroom to provide heat. Teachers, parents, and students would bring
ingredients for the soup. When this school finally managed to get a lunch room,
the principal had to go on a fund-raising drive to solicit the funds necessary to
buy the proper equipment for running the "lunch room."

One thing that was checked by the central office was the general upkeep and
sanitation of the buildings. As long as the buildings appeared to be in acceptable
condition, it did not really matter that the heating system, say, was not really
efficient. One principal said he frequently ended up having to stoke the furnace
himself to keep it running. One principal found, and this was no rare occurrence,
that after he and the others in the black community had knocked themselves out
working to get a bond issue passed for new facilities, the new school was for the
whites. All they were to get were two additional rooms. They had wanted an
auditorium and gymnasium, and the superintendent had had the architect draw
up the plans. But when it was presented to the board of education, it was
decided that the black school didn't need such facilities. What it really needed
was some more "pots and pans down there in that home economics room."

Another principal reported that he spent most of his time raising money to
buy things that were given to whites. Money had to be found for band
instruments, stage curtains, and playground equipment. Even most of the money
for the upkeep and improvement of school grounds had to be raised from
outside sources. And once money was found for upkeep and improvement, the
staff and students had to pitch in to help because custodial help was so unevenly
allocated.

Athletic programs were often as makeshift as the lunch programs. One
principal discovered to his dismay that the gap in funding was larger than he
realized when he later became principal of the integrated high school and gained
access to old records of funding for athletics. While his school had been
struggling along on a budget of about $1000 a year, the white high school had
had an athletics budget of $15,000. To supplement his small budget, he would
organize fund-raising drives. He found in his community that most of the money
raised came from the white merchants, although the black community did
contribute some too. As a result, though, of limited funds and facilities, his

school and many others like it could only offer a few sports. Basketball, which requires less space than most sports, was the major sport in black high schools. Many schools did not have football teams, but a large number had basketball teams. These teams were often the source of great pride, and if they were good enough, they competed in all-black statewide tournaments.

Extracurricular activities also suffered from lack of funds, not just in the school but in the community as well. A child who wanted to play in the band often would wait until the school could find some instrument, any instrument, for him to play, since his family was usually unable to provide him with one.

The principal was not only left alone in figuring out how to stretch what little money he did get, but he was often virtually given free rein in his selection of teachers. Where white principals in all-white schools had to accept those teachers selected by the superintendent's office, those teachers "recommended" (in reality, selected) by black principals for their high schools were almost always routinely okayed.

One principal recalled discovering the formula by which teachers were supposed to be allocated to each school. When he brought the fact that his school was understaffed to the attention of the superintendent, the superintendent admitted that it was and that such a teacher allocation formula existed. He agreed to do something about the situation, but tacked on an additional provision which claimed that the formula had to take into account the increase and decrease of the school population. The way the superintendent saw it, the population of the black schools would be declining in the future and, therefore, the number of additional teachers to be provided for the black school would not actually be the number that should have been allotted on the basis of the allocation formula alone.

The black principal often had no real idea what was going on at the white schools or what the general level of education there was. Often when the superintendent met with the black principal, he met with him alone, and the principal would have no idea what white principals were being told by the central office. These meetings were rare, and rarer still were visits to the schools from anyone in the central office. Quite frequently the central office was not even aware that black schools had yearbooks, and they cared little what was included in programs of instruction. Said one principal: "As long as we prepared you to dig a straight ditch and cook a good meal, and you didn't blow up the building . . . that was all they were concerned about."

But probably one of the most important aspects of the principal's role was the importance he had in the black community. In many areas he was the highest-paid black male and the one with the highest status. He was sometimes referred to as the "black mayor," and he was often the only link that his community had with whites. People would seek him out for advice—marital and financial.

One black principal decided to run for city council and found that even he did not know all the ins-and-outs of the whites' political games. He came in second (only eight votes behind the front runner) out of four for two possible council seats, only to find that he could not take office because of a technicality. He had gotten on the ballot, but he had only entered his name in the county and not also, as required, in the town book. Although he did not believe this information was purposely withheld from him and although he plans to run again, he still represented the man in the black community who would be most likely to know what goes on outside the black community.

Not only did black principals find themselves in the role of marital counselor and financial advisor, they often found themselves acting as "moneylenders," although when they lent others money they often knew they had no chance of getting it back. One principal said: "I don't know how much money that I would have if I could just think back on all that money that I gave." He would give families money for groceries, and occasionally he gave money even when he was pretty sure that was not what it was being used for. The principal also acted as a reference for many in his community. Many a family could get a loan only after the principal vouchsafed their reliability. And not only did he bail some out of jail; he "kept a whole lot out of them by speaking a good word for them."

The principal was included in the planning of almost everything the black community did. Many helped found credit unions and local boys clubs. He had to handle children with discipline problems, since the courts often turned such children back over to the principal for help. He was active in the black PTA, and he and black teachers would frequently visit the homes of students to talk with their parents. He kept the school building open long hours for students to have a place to study, and in general "the black school became the recreation facility, winter and summer." Parents used it for meetings and other community activities such as singing.

Interviews with Former Superintendents

One superintendent, speaking of the place of the black high school within the administrative district, stated: "While the school systems recognized the role and responsibility for educating all the children, it was clearly structured to be accomplished under a black-white dichotomy," so that even though by 1963-64 there were biracial principal and staff meetings, in terms of the curriculum, staffing and budgeting, the black and white schools were separate entities with very little overlap. Not all systems even went so far as to have regular biracial meetings, however. One superintendent told how his predecessor instituted a biracial meeting of all the principals "so that he could say publicly, 'Yes, the black and white principals are meeting together.' " There was only one meeting a year though, and it was very structured, with few questions and little participation by the black administrators. "They were there, but the only exchange took place between the white members." This, at least, was a definite step toward integration. A joint meeting of the principals in one district a few years before was described:

You had two tables that were about eight feet long where all the white principals sat, and about eight feet away there was a small table with two chairs for the Indian principals. Then farther on down the room there was another eight-foot table with the black principals. The superintendent sat with the white principals. They would turn in their textbooks and the black principals would pick up the ones which had just been turned back in, and the white principals would take the new ones.

The white principals did not seem to know much about what was happening in the black schools, in spite of the fact that they often said that they enjoyed a good relationship with the black administrators. One superintendent stated that when he was a principal he talked with black principals about common problems, and they attended each other's ball games, graduations, and other functions, yet he knew very little of the inner workings of the black schools until he became superintendent.

From the comments of the superintendents it would appear that the central administration involved itself very little with the operation of the black high school. The superintendents did not spend the same amount of time in the black schools as they did in the white schools. This was not because, as one superintendent put it, it was forbidden territory, but because "so much ado was made when a white superintendent went into the schools . . . that the white administrator felt like a visitor or a guest rather than a part of the system."

In theory, the superintendent and the board of education had the power to make all decisions regarding curriculum, staffing, and financing, but in many districts most of this was left up to the black principal. According to one superintendent, prior to desegregation, the allotment of funds was left up to the discretion of the superintendent, rather than being divided by a simple mathematical formula of so much per student per school. He recalled one particular case in which one black school received less than $.50 per student for instructional supplies, while some white schools received $5.00 or $6.00 per student.

The relationship of the black school and the central administration differed from unit to unit. In one administrative unit the school board appointed a five-to-seven member committee for each attendance district to run the schools in that district. Some schools had an advisory committee consisting of black parents. While the district committee had the power to select teachers, principals, and curricula, in general they were not really involved in the operation of the black schools. Rural systems often had a black supervisor appointed by the superintendent to represent the central administration. According to one superintendent, the supervisor was often mistrusted by the black principal, since any power play in decision making between the superintendent and the principal was carried out by the superintendent's representative, the supervisor.

The superintendents all agreed that the black principal was the most powerful force in the black high school and in the black community in most areas. For all practical purposes he was a black superintendent or assistant superintendent with the power to raise money, hire and fire personnel, and make recommendations regarding other black administrators in the district.

While the superintendent had the right to select the staff for the black schools, in most cases the principals would select their teachers "and it would be rubber-stamped by the superintendent." While the budget was determined by the superintendent, the black principal was given the freedom to raise whatever amount of money he thought appropriate. In fact, "he was the chief administrator. The relationship of the black principal to the superintendent was somewhat like the relationship of the superintendent to the board: only when you needed a policy, when you needed money, or when you had a problem were they called in."

The black principal handled most of the problems that arose by himself. If a problem existed, "the black principal would just be told that such and such a problem existed and then he would take care of it." It is interesting to note that some of the superintendents pointed out that these problems generally related to the mores of the town and were rarely about instructional problems, "since there was very little discussion about instruction back in those days." Black students and parents would not usually come to the superintendent with grievances and petitions, since "this would be a slam against the black administrator." The black principal regarded himself as the spokesman, and all complaints should go through him. "If there was someone complaining about the school and the teachers, he took it as a personal slam against himself, so he suppressed it himself."

The black principal was usually the highest-paid man, the high-status individual in the black community, and his power extended through both the school and the community as a whole. As one superintendent stated: "The faculty was pretty well dominated, the student body was dominated, and the parents were pretty well dominated."

Part of the black principals' power may have been related to the fact that they generally stayed on as principal for many years. This often resulted in their being the highest-paid principals in the entire school district. "They stayed for a number of reasons: They felt comfortable, it was normally their home, they were their own men, they enjoyed the prestige that they had in the community, and they enjoyed the freedom they had in the school." It is interesting to note that because the principal's salary was based on his degree certification, the number of teachers in his school, and the years of experience as a professional educator, often the black principal was the highest-paid public official in the area. This proved to be a continued irritant to important members of the white community who were knowledgeable about his actual salary.

The principal was really the unofficial community leader. With his backing a political candidate could be voted into office or an issue could gain support. Sometimes he used his influence indirectly by "letting someone else, maybe a teacher, community leader, or PTA representative be the spokesman . . . and you would know that when they were making statements . . . they may have been the mouthpiece of the principal."

With his power to employ not only professional personnel but also janitors, maids, and food-service workers, the black principal was often the largest employer of blacks in the community, and in a small town, he was one of the largest employers in the community as a whole. According to one superintendent, the black principal was often influenced by family ties and political considerations in making decisions regarding personnel.

I realized that it was sometimes political, and oftentimes the best qualified person was not chosen, but I was also smart enough to know that he's not really going to tell me the real reason he did it, and the real reason may be more important. . . . He would invariably get someone from a high social echelon if they were available because this gave him another hold for building a dynasty. In other words, if a daughter of an important person, let's say an undertaker, finished school, he would invariably hire this person because this would make another tie with the power structure in the community. There were very few individuals in 1963-64 who had any stronger power backing, and it was economic, it was political, and it was just leadership.

The principal himself had come up through the power structure. He got where he was because someone retired or stepped down and he was designated as heir to the throne. Once he became principal, he had the authority to recommend other blacks for administrative positions, but some superintendents thought that the black principal would be careful not to recommend anyone who would rival him. "He knew that if he recommended somebody, he was going to have to control him, so, in turn, he wasn't going to recommend anyone who might question him; if this guy got out of line, it was the principal who would have to straighten him out."

In spite of his apparent power, the black principal had all kinds of indirect pressures on him.

He had to play the ball game, too. He was probably more a part of the white power structure than of the black power structure, since in actuality there really wasn't any power with the blacks. The power was with the whites, and he knew it. You're talking about two individuals: the black principal as he operated within the black community and the black principal as he operated within the white power structure, almost as an "Uncle Tom."

With the advent of integration, the black principal was threatened by the possibility of losing his position of power and authority.

Threat of change is very upsetting to the man who has been running his own show, and he saw that instead of dealing as a separate person he was going to have to learn to deal with another whole community that he might or might not be able to control. I think that deep down inside many of the principals were fearful of integration because of the strength they had in a community with a segregated school.

Major Roles of the Black Principal

During the course of our study, we learned about many specific aspects of the different roles played by black high school principals in a variety of community and political settings. A composite view of the various roles played by the black high school principals provide a much clearer picture of his involvement as a professional educator. While one would be hard pressed to find a single individual black principal who played each of the roles to the extent described, our data suggest that the aggregate of black principals in the state did in fact perform these roles.

The Black Principal as a Superintendent

In addition to his specific duties as unit administrator, the black principal served as the black superintendent. His role as the black superintendent made him responsible for recruiting, hiring, and firing teachers. While the black principal's role in staffing his school was officially, with respect to the superintendent, an advisory one, there were few instances where the superintendent for the school system exercised more than a rubber stamp function in these matters. The black principal was expected to obtain funds for purchasing essential equipment to maintain and operate the school building, for purchasing all uniforms and equipment required to conduct extracurricular activities, for covering all expenses (travel, insurance, conference fees, etc.) associated with extracurricular activities and expenses (office and lounge furniture, clerical salaries and equipment, etc.) associated with operating the school. He was also expected to obtain funds to purchase books for the library and instructional materials for the classroom.

In his role as superintendent, the black high school principal set the policy for operating his unit, carried out all phases of staffing it, and solicited funds for the support of basic and extracurricular programs. The white superintendent carried out these functions for the white schools.

*The Black Principal as a
School Administrator*

The role of the black high school principal as a school administrator paralleled that of the white principal in a formal sense and informally exceeded it. In general, the black high school principal, like his white counterpart, was expected to assign teachers to groups of students, schedule classes and events, keep records on student attendance and movements, implement and monitor instructional offerings, maintain support supplies and materials, maintain facilities, fulfill requirements outlined in the school code (general administration), and work with parents on specific problems associated with school operations. Unlike his white counterparts, he was expected to carry out a program that required additional local financial support; for the white principal these funds were provided from tax sources. Therefore, in addition to his regular administrative duties, he had to spend about 30 percent of his time raising money to buy essential supplies for students and teachers, instructional and support equipment, transportation services for students, uniforms for extracurricular activities, and, in too many instances, books and other instructional materials for the library.

The black principal was also expected to raise all the funds necessary to staff his personal office with a secretary and to fill it with office equipment and supplies. Many of the principals reported that they had to raise a minimum of $10,000 per year just to operate their basic programs. In some instances, some principals stated that they had to raise at least $30,000 annually to operate a comprehensive secondary program for their black students. At first glance, $10,000 to $30,000 annually does not seem like a great deal of money. However, considering the income levels and the general economic conditions of the black communities these schools served, the feat was no small one. The fund-raising role of the black principal exacted its toll on him personally, as well as on the students, staff, and community he served as an educational leader.

The black principal spent about half of his time with housekeeping chores: compiling and organizing records, building maintenance (cleaning, repairs), routine inspections, reading and answering mail, and general administrative routine; and with pupil, personnel, and organizational problems. The time he devoted to certain duties changed according to his view of his accountability within the general limits placed on him by the superintendent. He spent about 20 percent of his time supervising instruction. However, much of this instructional supervision was indirect, because there was too much to be done and too many staff members to be observed for a black principal to complete this activity directly. Improvement in instruction depended largely on the nature of the staff and student population, and on the extent to which the principal was sensitive enough to recognize and develop those variables essential to effective instruction. There is little evidence to support a claim that the supervision of instruction by black principals was effective, because they were never allowed the luxury of having adequate time or resources to do the job right.

As an administrator, the black high school principal was expected to operate a comprehensive secondary program. However, he was only provided with a building (and elements associated with its maintenance), an instructional staff, and some books with which to complete the job. To a large extent his success in carrying out his official administrative duties depended very much on his success in carrying out his unofficial duties as fund-raiser. If a black principal failed to raise funds, the extent of his official administration was rigidly prescribed by the school code.

There is little doubt that many of the black principals were effective administrators, but one has to wonder how much more effective they might have been if they had not been saddled with the added responsibility of financing a program where the majority of their supporters and chief benefactors were themselves without adequate financial resources. Their effectiveness has to be studied and evaluated in the context of this confusion of educational and administrative roles and the expectations imposed on them.

The Black Principal as
a Supervisor

One of the specific duties of the black high school principal was to supervise all of the other black schools in the district. As the supervising principal for all black schools, he was expected to visit all schools in the district. During these visits he was expected to note problems and recommend solutions. When problems could not be solved locally, the black high school principal was responsible for calling the problems to the attention of the superintendent. In most instances all the black principals in the districts reported to the black high school principal, who in turn would make one report to the superintendent. Rarely would another black principal in the black high school principal's district go directly to the superintendent without his prior approval.

A great deal of the black high school principal's activity as supervisor was conducted during meetings of the School Masters Club, which was made up of black administrators in districts, regions, and statewide groups. At that time many of the problems encountered in the various buildings would be discussed and solutions would often be suggested. When the supervising principal visited other black schools in his district, it was mainly as a formality to check on how well solutions were working out rather than as an inspection tour to determine what problems existed.

Another responsibility of the black high school principal as a supervisor was to map bus routes, coordinate bus schedules, and select bus drivers for the district. Since buses were likely to make several stops at different schools in the district, the black high school principal had to see to it that the transportation of students was well coordinated with the requirements of the instructional program and the school code in each school unit. The black high school principal's concern with student transportation was directly tied to his over-all concern with the quality of the instructional program received by black children in his district.

The Black Principal as a Family Counselor

As a family counselor, the black high school principal heard arguments and suggested solutions to marriage problems as a regular matter of course. Many families testified that the black principal kept some marriages from breaking up. Juvenile delinquency problems were usually handled by the black high school principal as an extension of his role as an educational leader. On many occasions a word or recommendation from the black high school principal was sufficient to keep a black child from being prosecuted and sent to jail. The child was thus saved from being hampered by a permanent criminal record. Rarely would a plea on behalf of a youthful offender by a black high school principal fail to be honored if he agreed to assume responsibility for the child's conduct over a given period of time. The black principal could get these kinds of requests granted even when the parents of the youth in question could not do so.

The black principal also had to assume the role of chief spokesman for the community at funerals and many times had to preside over such affairs. He was also called on to settle property disputes that arose when people died intestate. The black principal was expected to advise families on the future educational and vocational choices of recent graduates. He was also expected to help families fill out important legal papers and forms, and to read and interpret important papers. In many instances, the black principal was expected to find employment for students and adults who were having difficulty in finding jobs. In short, the black principal was consulted on all kinds of personal problems that were not readily understood by members of his community, but that could critically affect the quality of their daily life. Given this situation, the black high school principal had to play the role of family counselor on many occasions, advising people on a wide range of social and personal problems.

The Black Principal as a Financial Advisor

The black high school principal was expected to be able to provide advice on the purchase of certain items for personal or professional use or on how money should be invested. He was expected to help people fill out income tax returns, write business letters, and formulate budgets. On many occasions he was asked to provide financial advice about the conduct of farm business and the purchase and sale of land. If someone in the black community came into a large sum of money, the black principal was almost always asked for advice on how to deal with it. In general, for almost every conceivable personal or business problem that a black community member might face, the black principal would be asked to serve as a financial advisor who would find reasonable solutions.

Since the black high school principal was often the highest-paid public employee (white or black) in the area, he exerted considerable influence as a financial advisor, because he had visible financial resources. On several occasions, black principals were instrumental in helping establish credit unions and cooperatives in black communities. The principal always played the pivotal role in getting these kinds of projects off the ground. In many instances the projects would not have survived had it not been for his financial advice and support.

The Black Principal as a Community Leader

As a community leader, the black high school principal was the unchallenged spokesman for the black community. He was expected to visit all black churches and give talks on topics of interest to members of the community. The black principal was the community's official host for welcoming visiting dignitaries and visiting groups. He was expected to provide suggestions and recommendations on how to deal with certain local political and social issues, including those issues affecting people over a much wider area. The black principal was also expected to introduce, explain, and interpret social and political trends affecting the black community. The position taken by the black principal on vital issues played a crucial role in the thinking and actions of the black community.

In his role as community leader, the principal was often asked to help with local elections and to drum up support for the passage of school bond issues and county bond issues (sewage, hospitals, streets, etc.). Many times these requests were in conflict with the black community's interests, because, even though they voted for passage of local bond issues, the new funds were not likely to be spent in their community. The black principal was in a tough spot on these issues, because he would violate one of his trusts if he failed to appear to favor the positive community development that passage of local bond issues represented.

Another aspect of the black high school principal's role as a community leader dealt with his participation in civic activities in the black and larger community. Often he was expected to coordinate the activities of different civic groups working together on a particular problem. In this role he was also expected to organize groups for political involvement, interpret local political issues, and design means for presenting grievances to the local white power structure. As a community leader, the black principal was expected to serve on local political and administrative boards, and to report the lack of specific services in the black community to the appropriate authorities.

In fulfilling his role as a community leader, the black high school principal looked more like an elected politician than a publicly paid educator. That accounts in part for the wide range of roles played by black principals as community leaders. It did not really matter whether the black principal acted as an agent of the black community or as an agent of the white power structure, he could not abdicate his responsibility to serve as a community leader, because the choice was not entirely his own.

The Black Principal as an Employer

In some of the eastern counties the black population exceeded the white population or was at least 40 percent of the total population. When this was the case, the black high school principal was often the largest single employer in the community. In some instances, the budget of the black high school was larger than any other budget in the whole county, because many areas did not have any local industry to rival its economic stature. As an employer, the black high school principal hired all the instructional staff, service personnel (janitors, maids, cooks, bus drivers, etc.), contractors for small repair jobs, office help, and special staff for special jobs. On many occasions, local high-school graduates and community people were employed by local industry as a result of recommendations provided by the black high school principal.

The Black Principal as a Politician

As a politician, the black high school principal was expected to serve as spokesman for the white community to the black community and vice versa. In his political role, the black principal was expected to be "the man" in both the white and black communities, and as such he was often the man in the middle. It was the black high school principal's responsibility to inform the white community what the black community was thinking and wanted. And in some instances, he was expected to influence the black community's thinking in one direction or another. Too often the black high school principal was asked to serve two masters with opposing requirements, opinions, and control. The white community exercised absolute control of material resources and job security, but the black community exercised control of the moral and spiritual values that governed his social action. The black high school principal had to exercise considerable political skill to remain a credible educational and community leader.

The black high school principal was usually asked to provide endorsements during all kinds of local elections, even when those running for office were openly hostile to the black community. During these times it took considerable skill to refuse without offending. The black principal was always the prime candidate for a political office requiring the appointment of a black citizen. Even when he did not take the appointment himself, only those recommended by him would be chosen to serve. The black principal was almost always put in charge of charitable fund-raising activities in the black community, such as Red Cross, United Fund, March of Dimes, etc. The white community also expected him to exercise a degree of control over the black community and its leaders. In short, the black high school principal was expected to be in control of all political activity being initiated by and affecting the black community. All of the principals agreed that failure to fulfill their roles as acceptable politicians resulted in strong reprisals from the white community and condemnation from the black community.

Background on the Black Principal

Of fifty-eight former principals of all-black high schools, 88 percent were born in North Carolina. Almost half of the principals (43 percent) grew up in rural areas, while 38 percent were raised in moderate-sized towns.

Fifty-nine percent of the principals had attended public undergraduate colleges in North Carolina, and 28 percent private undergraduate colleges in North Carolina. Ninety-three percent of the principals had obtained master's degrees, and 7 percent had only bachelor's degrees.

Almost half of the principals had had six to fifteen years teaching experience before becoming principal, 31 percent had had one to five years experience, and 9 percent had no experience. Thirty-two percent of the principals had served six to fifteen years as principal, and 10 percent had served more than thirty-six years. Most principals (58 percent) had served at only one or two different schools.

When asked about their status after desegregation, 55 percent of the principals reported that they kept the same position, while 10 percent moved to other schools, 5 percent became assistant principals, and 10 percent moved into administration at the central office. In addition, 66 percent reported on the questionnaire that they held this same position in 1973.

Table 5-1 shows that prior to desegregation the majority of principals earned less than $13,000 annually, while after desegregation over half earned more than $13,000 as principal. While no one had earned more than $16,000 annually

Table 5-1
Salaries of Principals Before and After Desegregation

| | Salaries of Principals Reporting | | |
| | Percent Before Desegregation | Percent After Desegregation | |
Annual Salaries	As Principals	As Principals	As Other Educa- tional Prof.
Under $5000			
$5000-5999	2		
$6000-6999	2		
$7000-7999	3	2	
$8000-8999	12	0	
$9000-9999	10	0	
$10,000-10,999	22	0	
$11,000-11,999	17	3	2
$12,000-12,999	14	9	3
$13,000-13,999	3	5	2
$14,000-14,999	3	5	2
$15,000-15,999	2	12	5
Over $16,000	0	31	2

before desegregation, nearly a third earned this much as principal after desegregation.

The H.V. Brown Schoolmasters Club

Black principals did not work in a vacuum. Because they were rarely, if ever, included in policy formation in the white power structure in their school administrative units, they formed their own group: the H.V. Brown School-masters Club. The club, which was formed in 1933 as an all-male professional schoolmasters organization under the leadership of H.V. Brown, then principal in Goldsboro, North Carolina, was known at first as the Pilots Club. Its general purpose was to help in the progress and orderly development of the school and the community, using all human and natural resources available. Anyone holding state academic qualifications who had received a bona fide appointment as principal of a school was qualified to become a member.

Over the years the club was extended to Craven, Duplin, Greene, Jones, Lenoir, Onslow, Johnson, Wilson, and Wayne counties, and it was renamed the H.V. Brown Schoolmasters Club. The purpose of the club widened, focusing on the principalship of the schools. It was felt at the time that with the increasing number of teachers and pupils, the principal should give more time to administration, curricula studies, teaching guides, rating scales, standardized tests, and other techniques. The club functioned to provide black principals with a forum for exchanging ideas, discussing new techniques, and sharing expertise. Principals would explain ways they had coped with certain problems in their schools as a way of suggesting courses of action for principals in other schools with similar problems.

The club, which is still in existence, brings outstanding speakers to local communities from the state department of public instruction, colleges and universities, and from the political arena. It encourages student scholarships and supports worthwhile community uplift projects. Meetings, which consist of luncheons held every third Wednesday of each month, rotate among the several counties in which the club's members are located.

The club provides public recognition for members when they retire as principals in the form of a public banquet with a featured speaker. At that time the retiring principal is presented with an engraved plaque. Many members who have retired as principals have gone on to be elected members of school boards; some help out with club activities part time; some serve on various advisory committees; others serve organizations as consultants.

6

The Black High School
Ten Years Later—1973

In previous chapters we have examined the black high school as it existed in 1963-64. During the ten-year period that followed, many changes were made in the public high schools of North Carolina as a result of both *integration* and *consolidation*. Many all-black high schools became elementary schools or junior high schools, or were closed entirely. Often a given school underwent several grade changes within that ten-year period. In some cases, when the school continued to operate, its name was changed.

Number of Schools and Principals

Data indicate that in 1963-64 ninety-one of the state's one hundred counties had at least one black high school and forty (44 percent) of these counties had one black high school. All of the counties had at least one white school, and only 13 of the counties had only one. In 1963-64 there were 493 white high schools and 226 black high schools, making a total of 719 public high schools. In 1973-74 the total number of public high schools was 366, or 353 fewer schools than there were ten years before.

In 1973-74, 25 percent of the counties had only one public high school, and 81 percent had five or fewer high schools, while in 1963-64 only 2 percent of the counties had only one public high school, and 43 percent had one to five high schools per county.

Only 58 of the 226 black high schools that existed in 1963-64 did not undergo changes in the grade levels they served. Many of the 168 schools in which grade changes were made had two or three grade changes after 1963-64. In addition to undergoing grade-level changes, some formerly all black high schools also had their school names changed. Thirty-two schools (14.2 percent) of the 226 schools had their names changed at least once during the ten-year period between 1963 and 1973.

As was indicated in a previous chapter, one of the characteristics of the black school was the tenure of its principals. Seventy-eight percent of the schools had only one or two principals between 1963 and 1973. Only 15.9 percent had three different principals, 4.9 percent had four different principals, and .9 percent had five different principals during the ten year period.

Black High School Principals in 1973

In 1963-64, of the 226 principals of black schools that included high school grades, twenty-four served as principals of senior high schools (grades 9-12 or 10-12), twenty-three served as principals of junior-senior high schools (grades 5-12, 6-15, 7-12, or 8-12), and the remaining 179 served as principals of union high schools (grades 1-12). Ten years after, there were fifteen black principals serving in schools with grades 10 and/or above. Of this number, one served as a principal of a tenth-grade school, and one as a principal of ninth- and tenth-grade school. The principals were located in fourteen different counties and fifteen different administrative units.

Closing of Black High Schools

By 1973, ninety-three of the 226 formerly all black high schools had ceased to operate altogether. Two-thirds of these schools closed between 1968 and 1970. Of these schools, only 63 still contained students in grades 9-12 during the last year of the school's operation. Twenty-five schools operated their last year with elementary school students (grades 1-8), and five schools had only grades 5-9 or 7-9. The largest percentage of schools closed before 1973 (44.1 percent) were those with grades 1-12.

Of the formerly all-black high schools still in operation in 1973, 120 had ceased to operate as high schools. In short, by the fall of 1970, 87.5 percent of the schools that had been black high schools in 1963-64 and were still open in 1973 were no longer functioning as high schools. Again, 1968, 1969, and 1970 seem to be the years in which most of these formerly all black schools ceased to operate as high schools. Thus, in the fall of 1970 only forty formerly all-black high schools were still operating as high schools, and by the fall of 1972 this number was reduced to only thirteen.

Changes in Extracurricular Experiences

Data for this area is spotty and very difficult to obtain accurately. Part of the difficulty lies in the sensitivity of the problem in areas that have struggled through desegregation issues and fights in the recent past. Another part of the difficulty is related to the fact that specific data on black student participation in extracurricular activities are no longer kept. However, yearbook analysis provide some interesting insights into the problem.

Without doubt, there has been a qualitative change in the depth and breadth of the type of extracurricular activities black youth experience in desegregated schools. For example, in 1963-64, looking at black high schools as a group, there was a total of forty-three different extracurricular activities in which students could participate. More than half of all black high schools had twenty-four of these activities in their school, and only 25 percent of the schools reported that they had fewer than twelve of the activities in their schools. Table 6-1 shows that in 1972-73 senior high schools had a variety of activities for student participation ranging from thirty to fifty-nine different activities, with an average of forty-two activities per school. The percentages of students participating in each school is probably less than indicated by absolute count, because many students participate in a number of different activities. Black students who participate in activities make up 20 percent to 50 percent of the total number of students involved, with an average participation of 31 percent. In each of the six schools used, the pattern of black student participation across the various activities differed widely. Twenty-six percent of the staff assigned to work with student groups in the six schools was black. The staff members served in a restricted number of activities.

Changes in Staff Assignments

In the six senior high schools we selected for study, 24 percent of the administrators and support staff in the six schools were black. Five of the principals were white, and two were black. There were seven white and three black assistant principals in the six schools. Twenty-nine percent of the teachers in the six schools surveyed were black. Even though there has been a decided drop in the percentage of black administrators, the percentage of black teachers (29 percent) in the six schools selected is greater than the percentage (24.8 percent) of black teachers in the state in 1963-64.

Table 6-1
Selected Characteristics of Student Activity Patterns in Six Senior High Schools—1972-73

Schools	Enrollment	Number of Different Activities	Total No. of Students Participating	Percent	Black Students Participating		Number of Activities Without Black Students	Staff Assigned to Various Activities	
					No.	Percent		Total	Black
1	2080	44	1183	57	234	20	13	20	2
2	1666	35	758	45	241	32	4	14	2
3	1044	41	938	94	326	33	5	44	11
4	1659	30	472	28	236	50	3	22	7
5	1476	45	900	61	235	26	3	21	8
6	1378	59	1196	87	325	27	9	12	4

Table 6-2
Selected Characteristics of Administrators and Staff in Six Senior High Schools 1972-73 School Year

Schools	Administrators and Support Staff		Administrators				Teachers Number of		
			Principals		Asst. Principals				
	Total	Black	White	Black	White	Black	Total	Blacks	Percent
1	15	2	1		1	1	96	17	18
2	9	2	1		1	1	70	23	33
3	19	3	1		1	1	52	13	25
4	12	7	1	1	1		78	28	42
5	11	1	1		2		75	27	36
6	10	3		1	1		60	12	20
Total	76	18	5	2	7	3	420	120	29

7 Inferences and Propositions for Further Consideration

The black high school in North Carolina was a direct and positive force in the development of the community it served. It provided leadership and participation opportunities for black staff, students, and laymen when no other official institution was available to serve this community. *As far as we can determine, the black high school was the only long-term publicly supported institution that was pervasive across the black community, and that was controlled, operated, staffed, populated, and maintained by blacks that has ever existed (or most probably will ever exist again) in the United States.*

All high schools serve their respective communities. Most high schools, however, serve their communities indirectly, because they help to define those choices that students might make in fulfilling their roles as citizens in the larger community. In this sense, high schools provide the foundation for later choices, but play only an indirect role in the specific choices individual students make regarding their lives. The role of the black high school in the black community was central to its functioning, and because of this it served its community more directly than the white high school did its community. The black high school seemed to play a critical role in determining the opportunities available to members of the black community, more so than was the case with the white high school in the white community. Without the presence of the black high school, the black community would have been severely limited educationally, socially, politically, and economically. There were few if any educational opportunities for black citizens outside the black high school. Most social events in the black community could not have taken place if the black high school had not existed. It was expected by the members of both the black and white communities that the politics within and outside the black community would be a central concern of the black high school and especially of the principal of the black high school. Lastly, a great deal of the economic activity in the black community was dependent on the presence and support of the black high school. In many ways, the black high school played a crucial role in defining, directing, and creating major social functions in the black community. Black communities would have been unable to carry on many activities critical to their development, and they would not have been exposed to ideas and issues that enabled their members to take advantage of existing opportunities or enabled them to pursue newly created opportunities. The black community needed the black high school to carry out its social functions. In that sense, the black community was almost completely defined by the scope of the black high school.

73

The white high school's role in the white community was much different than that played by the black high school in its community. While the white high school did contribute to the educational, social, political, and economic life of the white community, it did not control these major social functions. In fact, these major social functions were controlled so totally by other parts of the white community that the vast majority of white high schools would not have dared to go beyond supporting those values and ideals that were specified by the white community as being properly the role of the school. In addition, much critical education could only be gained in the white community outside the high school. Unlike the black community, the white community dictated the social learnings that the white high school could offer. The social pattern of the white community was not set directly by the white high school. Typically, the white high school was expected to be and remain apolitical in its community activities. The political activities were controlled by the white community outside the white high school. The white high school played a minor role in the economic life of the white community.

Little influence could be exerted by the white high school on the white community because the white high school was dependent on the white community for its economic base, whereas the black community was dependent, to a large degree, upon the black high school for its economic base. Thus, the economic relationship between the black high school and the black community was often the reverse of the relationship observed in the white community.

While the white community might choose to deal with the black community directly, it almost always included the black high school in its deliberations. However, many times the white community dealt only with the black high school as the representative of the black community. The white high school hardly ever made any contact with the black community outside the black high school. The black high school was the bridge, the communication link between the black and white communities.

The kinds of development experienced by most black communities in North Carolina can be directly tied to the influence of some aspects of the black high school's program. In the majority of instances the black high school offered the only avenue to the outside world for most black citizens. Since the black high school controlled much of the information coming into the black community from the outside, it exerted a great influence over the members of that community. The black high school also served to open doors and create opportunity for blacks within and outside the black community. In a real sense then, the black high school *was* the black community in many areas in North Carolina. This being so, the extent of progress a given black community could make was dependent on the course taken and the programs implemented by the black high school.

The Black High School as
a Social System

Social system, as we are using the term, must not be confused with the notion of society, or the notion of state, or thought of as only being applicable to large aggregates of human interaction in conducting social functions. With reference to the black high school, social system deals with functions of the black high school as an institutional unit within a given community, which may also be thought of as a social system.

Viewing the black high school as a social system provides a general framework for understanding how the school served its students and the black community in particular and the total community in general. This framework should enable us to put forth inferences and propositions concerning the black high school and its effects on community development.

Financing Education

Inference 1: *Educational policy involving financial support made at the top and directed at a specific problem causes many problems and conflicts at lower levels that were not intended or foreseen.*

The above inference was arrived at as the result of seeing the turmoil caused at the state and local school levels when the Congress of the United States authorized the federal treasury in 1836 to distribute funds for the support of local educational efforts on the basis of state population. This was the first congressional effort to provide financial support for local educational efforts. These funds did not carry any stipulation for social application outside of aiding local communities in their efforts to educate their youth. Yet the requirement that distribution be based on federal population, which included black slaves, caused a split between the white citizens in eastern and western North Carolina that persisted for more than a decade. The conflict was caused by the method of distribution stipulated. The legal method for distributing state funds for local educational efforts was based on the distribution of the white population. Conversely, the legal method of distributing the federal funds provided to the state by the Congress was based on the federal population of the state, which included black slaves. Since eastern North Carolina had more black slaves than whites in their population, they got more than twice as much of the federal allocation for the education of each white child. In contrast, there were few, if any, black slaves in western North Carolina, so that local educational units in this section of the state received less than half the amount of federal funds for each white child than was awarded to their counterparts in the east. This was seen by North Carolinians in the west as being unfair and unlawful according to state practice and law.

Any policy decisions at one level concerning a specific problem area in an educational unit can cause problems and conflicts in areas that were not the intended target. This is related to the fact that policy changes the roles of certain individuals in a social system. A change in the roles of some individuals in a social system changes the roles of other individuals in that social system. Life can never be the same for anyone in that social system. When the change comes, some will lose ground and others will gain, because the relationship between the various roles have changed to meet the new demands of the new policy.

The policy to desegregate the dual school system in North Carolina produced profound changes in the lives of the staff, students, and parents who made up the social system of the black high school. The roles that characterized life for individuals in the black high school were eliminated when schools were integrated. Behavior patterns that were effective in the black high school were no longer functional and success-producing in the desegregated schools. In the beginning, many conflicts resulted from individuals in the desegregated high school not knowing what their role expectations were. Many of the expulsions and suspensions of black students that occurred immediately after desegregation (and which still occur with a high degree of frequency in too many schools in some areas) were the direct result of changed role expectations created by the policy to desegregate schools.[1] Until the desegregated school learns to accommodate the different role expectations of those it serves and who serve it, or to change its role expectations so that they complement each other, the conflict will continue and everybody will lose: the student, the staff, the community, and the nation as a whole.

The impact of policy changes on the social system of a school is so critical to the quality of the experiences that students, staff, and pupils can receive that the subject warrants more careful study than has been the case to date. Without such thoughtful and systematic consideration, high schools will continue to deteriorate and fail to serve students and society, and any attempt to alter their ill-fated course by making cosmetic changes in curricula offerings, inservice training, and human relations sessions will be unsuccessful. The social dynamic that characterizes too many high schools in America today cries out for a forceful and quick redirection of effort.

Proposition 1: *New policy creates role inconsistency in social systems expected to implement that policy.*

Allocation and Distribution of Funds

Inference 2: *When funds are allocated for educational services they are based on aggregated data; however, the distribution of educational services are determined by disaggregated data.*

Support for this inference resulted from our observation of state allocation of funds to local school districts on a per student basis to buy specific educational services. For example, the state provided $3.99 per student to each school district for the purchase of library materials and supplies. Our data reveal that 71.8 percent of all-black high schools spent less than that amount, and 29.5 percent spent less than half the state's allocation. The remaining 28.2 percent of the black high schools reported that they spent more than the state allocation ($3.99) per student for library materials and supplies. This funding was intriguing, because the state reported that $3.99 was allocated and spent on library materials and supplies for each student.

Interviews with former black principals and white superintendents provided some interesting insights into the problem. The black principals indicated that many times they did not receive any funds from the local superintendent for library materials and supplies. Whenever they received these funds, they were often only a fraction of the state allocation per student. In the main, black principals reported that they themselves were expected to raise money to purchase library materials and supplies for their schools. Some of the white superintendents revealed how these state allocated funds were distributed locally. The general formula followed by some superintendents was ten to one. That is, ten times more of the available money was spent on the white student than on the black student for library materials and supplies. Using the state allocation per student as the base figure, $7.18 for each white student and $.80 for each black student would be provided locally for the purchase of library materials and supplies. However, the biennial reports published by the state indicated that $3.99 per student was spent for the purchase of these educational services. Clearly, the black student failed to receive what the state had allocated even though published state data suggested that he received his share.

We believe that this is not an isolated incident and that this practice is still quite common. Certain students in school receive far fewer educational services than were allocated for them, and furthermore, the system of accountability does not reveal this discrepancy. It is our thinking that as long as there is confusion on the nature and adequacy of data for making certain kinds of decisions, accountability for allocating funds cannot be determined by the tax-paying public that makes these funds available for use on all children. When local school systems aggregate data on money spent per student it is easy for the public to be misled into believing that each student received the same amount of educational services. Therefore, the public can be easily deceived into thinking that an educational service was purchased for each student when this was not the case. As long as data are presented in this way, it will not be possible to establish any standards of accountability for educating specific groups of students served by the school. Unless the public is provided with a means to compare the amount of money allocated with the amount of educational services actually received by each student, it will remain impossible to judge whether the school is serving the public it is supposed to serve.

Proposition 2: *The aggregation of data serves to facilitate some educational decisions and to distort others.*

Purposes of Social Systems

Inference 3: *A social system serves many purposes that are further reaching than the goals conceptualized for that system.*

The black high school as an institution was given a specific social function in its community in particular and in the society in general. It was expected that the black high school would provide educational services for black youth within the general framework of community expectations and the particular requirements of the state school code. Community expectations and legal requirements defined the black high school as an institution with a specific social function in society. In attempting to fulfill its expected social function in society, the black high school operated as a social system with a wholeness and pulse beat geared to serve those inside and outside its direct influence. The black high school as a social institution had to deal with the role interactions and personal opportunities afforded individuals who were affected by the system.

One example of the black high school's influence as a social system is evident in the role and opportunities of the black principal. Our data revealed that the black high school principal played a variety of leadership roles within and outside the black community. As the administrative and perceived leader of the black high school, the black principal became visible to the larger community, which in turn made him attractive for fulfilling other roles. Likewise, if the black high school principal chose to stay in the black high school he still had high status, community acceptance, psychological support, meaningful activities to perform, and value as a person. As a social system, the black high school offered the black high school principal a choice between these equally attractive options. Without the presence of the black high school, this kind of opportunity and choice of options would not have been available on a broad basis for a large number of black professionals.

Another example of the influence of the black high school as a social system is associated with the leadership and apprenticeship opportunities it offered black students, staff, and laymen. In the first instance, black students were expected to fill leadership and apprenticeship positions that occurred naturally as part of the operational components of the black high school. Leadership and apprenticeship opportunities in organized extracurricular activities offered real and meaningful roles that enabled black students to participate in an activity that enabled them to practice skills that were directly transferable to fostering effective work in the community and during adulthood. Since the roles black students filled were real, personally meaningful, and an integral part of the social system characterizing the black high school, these students learned a great deal more about themselves and their abilities than would have been possible through the content program of the curricular system of the school alone, and they were able to be successful in the psychologically supporting system that the black high school provided. This made them more likely to achieve success in other social systems encountered later in life. The black high school as a social system represented a training community for black students, because it provided them with some of the opportunities to practice certain skills and attitudes that would have been unavailable to them in the larger community. For the black student in North Carolina this kind of experience was likely to exert a profound influence on his chances and choices throughout his life.

When the staff of the black high school are viewed as members of a social system, their roles gain a deeper meaning for them personally and a broader scope professionally. Since the staff was directly responsible for implementing, operating, maintaining, and ensuring the quality of curricular and extracurricular programs, they were afforded opportunities to learn things that lay outside their special field of study or specific instructional assignment. The staff was responsible for helping students learn the roles required to conduct both the curricular and extracurricular program of the school. It was the responsibility of the staff to communicate and teach students both formally and by example the rules of procedure, traditional practice, and community standards governing what was expected of students performing certain roles. This requirement made it possible for the staff of the black high school to become involved with students officially on a total person-to-person basis. The guidance the staff offered students was closely tied to a summary evaluation of their talents, desires, and values, because it resulted from an evaluation of students' activities in a variety of behavior settings formed over a long period. This fact made staff members of the black high school keenly aware of the match between the personal characteristics of the students and the opportunities available to them in the community and the larger world. The staff's role in providing guidance for students was a natural outgrowth of the curricular and extracurricular activities they experienced in common with their students. The black high school was a total experience for its students.

The black high school also offered staff members a broader experience than their specific instructional assignments by providing opportunities to participate in meaningful leadership and apprenticeship roles necessary for the operation of the school. Opportunities to head departments, assist others in managing complex activities, chair committees, head and administer special fund drives, coordinate community related activities, and participate in professional organizations at the local, state, and national levels were available to any staff member if he was interested. The black high school offered staff members many opportunities for leadership experiences enabling them to gain personal status within and outside the school, to have meaningful and rewarding involvement, and to achieve personal advancement within and outside the school. The black high school as a social system made it possible for staff members to fulfill personal aspirations as an integral part of their professional responsibility. This made the black high school a personal experience as well as a professional one for its black staff.

The black high school as a social system involved the black layman in meaningful and useful ways. Black laymen participated in fund-raising drives, cooperative organizations (PTA, Parent Committees, etc.), social and civic organizations, (fraternities, sororities, United Way, etc.) and specialized clubs sponsored by the school to support its programs and other programs in the community. The key to layman participation in terms of the black high school was related to the fact that the activity in question involved the school and its occupants as a precondition for success and as such could be an extension of the school's program or an aid to the community-based activity. One of the values of lay participation in school-related or associated programs and activities is the opportunity it afforded laymen to participate in shaping, guiding, and operating the activity in question. Laymen could serve in leadership positions and deal with significant community and school problems in cooperation with the black high school staff. The black layman felt himself to be an integral part of the school's programs and problems. While black laymen felt obliged to support the black high school's programs, they also thought of themselves as a significant factor in finding solutions to problems that involved them. Since the black layman had complete access to the facilities and staff of the black high school, he was provided with a meaningful setting for involvement and learning new skills. As a consequence, the black layman felt that he was an intimate and integral part of the school and its program.

Proposition 3: *If there are meaningful opportunities for individuals to become involved in significant roles, these individuals will gain additional and transferable skills that contribute directly to personal and community development.*

Group Socialization

Inference 4: *When two groups who were socialized or expected to be socialized in different social systems are combined, the social system of one group will prevail as the social system to be followed by both groups. Therefore, the social system for the combined groups represents a familiar and supportive environment for one group and a new and alien environment for the other group. This causes one group to experience an environment that is "balanced," while the other group experiences an environment that is "imbalanced."*

As long as the black student knew what was expected of him and acted to fulfill that role expectation, the social system of the black high school was an environment with environmental balance for him. The same was true for the white student in his school environment. In order to provide the reader with a better picture of how black and white students' role expectations and actions were in concert with the environmental balance of their respective schools, examples involving both students will be presented in parallel form.

Our first example deals with the enforcement of dress regulations. Many black male students like to wear hats that are colorful and unusual in some way. While the black high school had regulations against wearing hats inside the school building, any male student seen wearing one would be calmly asked to remove it and in most instances the student would comply. However, it was not unusual for the same student to put his hat back on his head once he was not in the presence of the staff member who asked him to remove his hat. When a black student was seen a second time with his hat on, he was reminded to remove his hat as calmly as he was the first time around. There was hardly any threat of punishment, because the offense was not considered a major one. In short, the role expectation regarding hat wearing inside the school building was known and accepted by the staff and students, and the degree of force used to make students comply with regulations concerning the wearing of hats inside the school building was tempered by the amount of seriousness staff members placed on the offense in terms of the school's purpose.

A white male student would not be allowed to wear his hat inside the white high school, and he would be expected not to. If he did, that would represent a breach of school regulations. If a white student was observed wearing his hat indoors he was likely to be given a stern lecture by a staff member concerning his disrespect for school rules and regulations and for his fellow students and associates in the school. Along with the reprimand, a white student just might be given a strong warning that promised definite reprisals if he were again observed exhibiting the same behavior. Many times a notation on the student's record might be made so that a second offense would be treated according to the reprisals promised at the time of the first offense. If a white student were observed by the same staff member engaging in the same behavior, he was almost certain to be punished or suspended, since he would be seen as lacking personal discipline and as being disrespectful to the school's practices and regulations. For this he would be punished and his parents would be involved in answering for such unbecoming and unexpected behavior on the part of the student. In the white school this was a serious offense.

The two examples discussed above show how similar behaviors by different students attending different high schools in the same school system are viewed and interpreted differently because the social systems of the two schools demand different role expectations. In the black high school, hat wearing was thought of as a relatively minor offense and consistent with the life style of the students. Though rules governing hat wearing in the black school were enforced, few staff would agree that this behavior was serious enough to warrant strong reprimands or punishment. The social system of the black high school accommodated the life styles of the students it served and the role expectations of all participants were seen in this light. The environment of the black high school was balanced for the black student and in harmony with his life style with regard to role expectations, just as the white student in the white high school had a role expectation consistent with his life style.

After the black and white high school were desegregated, the social system of the "integrated" school in many instances did not serve either group consistently or well. In most instances one social system that was consistent with the life styles of one group became the official environmental setting for all participants in the school. This immediately represented a situation of imbalance for the group of participants whose life styles were not considered in the social system of the "integrated" high school. Let us return to the hat wearing example. The vast majority of the "integrated" high schools in North Carolina took on the social system of the former white high school as the basis for determining the role expectations of all school participants. For the white student, rules dealing with wearing hats inside the school represented business as usual. On the other hand, these hat wearing rules represented a completely different reality for many black students, and for them the new social system of the school was inconsistent with their life styles and preconceived expectations. The social system of the "integrated" school was consistent with the role expectations of the white student but not with the role expectations of many of his black counterparts. As a result, many black students were expelled or suspended for infractions that would have been considered minor in the black high school. This phenomenon is documented in *The Student Pushout*, published by the Southern Regional Council and the Robert F. Kennedy Memorial. A representative sample of the problems are presented here to illustrate how various students were affected in many southern school districts after the desegregation of schools.

School officials and community leaders often have widely different explanations for suspensions and expulsions and the disparity between the numbers of blacks and whites subjected to those actions. Yet sometimes they agree. And sometimes, the official viewpoint reveals underlying attitudes.

The official reasons, the immediate causes given for most suspensions or expulsions, are common in every state and school district and are echoed in the words of nearly every school official. The reason most often assigned is given a number of different labels—disrespect for authority, insubordination, or disobedience. Other, somewhat less common reasons listed are fighting, gambling, possession of weapons, use of intoxicants, smoking, truancy, habitual violation of rules, and excessive tardiness.

While students' comments revealed support for order and rules to maintain order, young people sharply criticized (1) the arbitrary nature of the rules; (2) the unequal application of them, including what they viewed as open discrimination; (3) the misuse of authority; and (4) the failure of teachers and administrators to see and understand deeprooted personal, social, and other factors which cause misbehavior.[2]

Our study of the black high school revealed that the rules governing black students in black schools could be criticized for the same reason offered in the case of "integrated" schools. However, the difference for the black student was related to the enforcement and the perception of the enforcement of the rules by school officials. Since human judgment plays such a crucial role in the enforcement and application of school rules to student behavior, the person charged with the responsibility for making those judgments determines the social system that is to be honored and the nature of the ecological environment of the school. In most instances, black students in "integrated" schools felt that white authority was arbitrarily imposed and that they were most likely to suffer as a result. For the black student the environment of the "integrated" school was imbalanced and alien to his life style. There was always confusion between the "rules of governance" and the "application of these rules" for the black student in the "integrated" school. This appeared not to have been generally the case when black students attended black high schools.

Further reading in *The Student Pushout* reveals more concrete examples that are helpful in giving a more complete picture of the environmental press affecting black students in newly desegregated high schools.

The rules and variation of them seem endless as causes leading to suspension or expulsion, as the students view them. They include a host of minor infractions, such as "cutting lunch line," "having a cigarette on me," "wearing another girl's gym suit," "smoking," "leaving a tray on the lunchroom table," "cursing," "not putting in my shirt tail," and "not having tennis shoes for P.E."

Especially in newly desegregated schools what seem like minor infractions may lead to big explosions. Often, in the first stages of desegregation, suspicions are widespread and tempers hot. Real or imagined fear of harassment can keep the threats of violence simmering and one minor brush with authority can mark a student for later discipline.[3]

A quick review of the infractions noted shows that the importance placed on each one is highly subject to human judgment and social preference. In some instances, school authorities have no legal right to enforce rules (dress codes, etc.). Our study of the black high school revealed that many of the infractions noted above would have been treated as minor and dealt with accordingly by mutual agreement between the staff member and the student. This change in role expectations and rule enforcement styles and preferences created great difficulty for large numbers of black students in newly desegregated schools.

When black students were asked about some of the environmental changes they encountered in newly desegregated schools, they revealed specific details that enable us to make a more precise comparison with their experiences in the black high school. In the newly desegregated high schools:

According to student reports, the most numerous offenses leading to suspensions or expulsions are fighting among students and conflict with leaders and administrators.

Here again the list of causes is almost as long as the roll of students interviewed: conflict with principal . . . disagreement with teacher . . . speaking opinion . . . argument . . . didn't want teacher if she moved me out of the seat, she should move white people too . . . teacher accused the student of saying something he didn't say . . . disrespect for the teacher . . . threatening a teacher . . . talking smart . . . pushing teacher when pushed . . . talking in class . . . laughing in class . . . disobeying classroom rules . . . not bringing books . . . not obeying orders . . . not working . . . not writing the preamble to the Constitution . . . not co-operating . . . not turning in Senior proofs . . . not doing school work . . . not having money for pictures.

Student activists are obvious targets of discipline, some for clear reasons, some for questionable cause; being a leader in a walk out . . . wearing a black arm band . . . boycotts . . . sit-ins.[4]

In the black high school student behaviors that were treated as major infractions in the desegregated school generally occurred too infrequently and were too minor to be of great concern or to warrant official systematic corrective action. Our data suggest that the behavior of black students in the desegregated high school was essentially unchanged from the behavior they exhibited while attending the black high school. The black student responded in relation to the expectations of the school and the actions of the staff. When there was an abrupt change in the expectations and actions of the staff in the desegregated school, the black student's responses were not synchronized with the social system of the school he now attended, and this new environment presented him with an imbalanced social structure. Until the environment of the school acquires an environmental balance for the black student, he will continue to remain outside the social system of the school he attends. Therefore, black students will be systematically deprived of the opportunity to become an integral part of the prevailing social system and to learn those skills that are greater and further-reaching than those skills associated with the formal instructional program of the school. Since black students previously had the experience of participating fully in the black high school, it is a great loss to the black student today if the schools he attends operate on the basis of a social system that denies him access to a total learning experience. If the social system of a particular school fails to support a given student's aspirations, needs, and desires, written rules of procedure will be of little help, because rules of procedure are ultimately translated in terms of the prevailing social system.

Proposition 4: *The ultimate utility of the school for a given student is dependent upon the extent to which the school's social system represents a balanced environment for him.*

Study of Public Education

Inference 5: *The study of one segment of public educational practice is necessarily tied to the study of public education in general.*

The black student experienced a total involvement in the life of the black high school and performed those roles that enabled the school to conduct a full program of curricular and extracurricular activities. The black student in the black high school could aspire to hold any leadership or apprenticeship position that was available. He was limited only by the strength of his individual determination and talents. In addition, there were many choices opened to him for personal involvement in meaningful activities. Most of the students' activities in black schools involved members of the black community, because the activities represented the opportunities available for improving the quality of life for the whole community at the time and in the future. The black community saw the black high school as an instrument for the development and improvement of their youth in particular and raising the level of existence in the black community in general. Our study clearly showed that the black community's fate in North Carolina was tied to that of the black high school. The black community had a crucial stake in working and fighting for the survival of the black high school as an institution geared to their needs and opportunities.

When the black high school is viewed in terms of public education, we can observe how the goals of society can be met in a specialized setting. Even though the specialized setting may be generally unknown to the total population, goals can be attained that serve the total population. In addition, that specialized setting may tend to serve the actual participants more effectively as a total experience than would be the case in an institutional setting that purported to provide the same service without reference to the particular characteristics of those being served. Therein lies one justification for rating the black high school as being extremely effective in carrying out the mandates of public education.

The black high school did a credible job in fulfilling the charges outlined by the state for providing public education, and it provided as well a much broader experience for youth, thus contributing directly to the development of the black community. Leadership, apprenticeship, and participation opportunities provided by the black high school for black staff, students, and laymen helped to develop the community's capability to act on its own behalf. The black high school also made it possible for black citizens, young and old, to practice and develop in a realistic laboratory those skills that were required to better the conditions of their lives. Since opportunities to practice and develop these skills were not widely or generally available in other institutions in the local black community, the black high school filled a void. For that reason the black high school was a vital experience in the life of the black community and contributed immeasurably to the progress recorded in many of these communities over the years they existed.

Proposition 5: *Since problems in public education are interrelated, the conduct of one well-defined segment of educational practice is reflective of the conduct of the total enterprise.*

Operational Consequences of Policy Formation

Inference 6: *Legal mandates and policy formations directed at integration contributed directly to the consolidation of schools in a number of local communities. School consolidation problems may have contributed as much to the administrative difficulty of high schools as did the desegregation of schools.*

Most of the research on school desegregation problems centers on either the legal or the attitudinal components of the issues and problems associated with the effectiveness of the school. Such things as equal access, fair treatment, student interaction patterns, individual psychological states (self-concept, personal involvement, etc.), and geographic and demographic relationships to educational outcome tend to shape the majority of the research studies involving school desegregation. Very little, if any, research is focused on the structural changes that occur in certain areas as a by-product of school desegregation. This oversight is partly related to the complexity of the interaction of critical variables that are not usually taken into account as a starting point for initiating educational research.

The demographic patterns in states that had *de jure* school segregation as opposed to *de facto* school segregation were much different, and those differences alter drastically the shape of school desegregation and its effects on the structure of school programs. The majority of high schools were located in small towns that ordinarily would have required only one school to house all grades. In addition, most of these towns had a black population that lived in many areas throughout the area in question. Segregation in the South was primarily confined to social areas and did not include physical proximity as a prime factor in determining residence. Blacks and whites tended to live close by each other in most areas in North Carolina and throughout the South. These demographic factors had a profound influence on the structural shape of high schools in North Carolina after school desegregation.

The first structural effect was that most of the towns in North Carolina that had two high schools (one white and one black) ended up with one high school after school desegregation. In many instances the school population of the local high school facility more than doubled in size. This represents a structural change for the local school's programs and practices, in addition to the social and traditional changes inherent in school desegregation. Few professionals in

North Carolina had had any prior experience in administering or working in schools of the size that schools became overnight in North Carolina. According to Barker and Gump, the size of a high school can have profound effects on the behavior of students.[5] Therefore, *many of the school problems* attributed to attitudinal and social problems between students, between students and staff, and between staff can be explained in part by factors related to changes in the size of the school population. To continue to explain or associate school output (achievement, student participation, life success, etc.) only in terms of attitudinal and social interaction problems is to restrict one's explanatory power to factors that do not account for much of the observed variance. Further research in this area must take into account size as a variable in the study of desegregated schools in North Carolina and in the South.

In 1963-64 only 7.5 percent of the administrative units had one high school; by 1973-74 the percentage of administrative units with one high school increased to 45.6 percent. In addition, there was a reduction in the total number of high schools in the state from 719 in 1963-64 to 366 in 1973-74, an elimination of 353 high schools in North Carolina. These two factors related to school consolidation (increased school size and reduction in the number of schools) tended to profoundly affect the programs and practices of the public high schools in North Carolina. Public high schools after desegregation became much more complex in their organizational structure, and the scope of their programs were broadened considerably. New roles dictated by these structural changes affected staff, students, and laymen alike. To attribute the black community's distance and estrangement after desegregation to social and attitudinal factors associated with school desegregation rather than to factors of size may have been a grave error on the part of educational researchers. Such errors may have been instrumental in focusing the attention of policy-makers on the wrong factors as they tried to work out some of the problems that appeared in high schools immediately after school desegregation.

Proposition 6: *Structural changes in schools have a greater impact on the nature of program and practices and on the resulting outcomes than do social and attitudinal factors, which themselves are often a result of structural changes.*

School Experience of Youth

Inference 7: *The school experience of black and white youth was altered greatly as a result of desegregation. A greater number of students appear to have previously obtained a broader exposure to certain kinds of experiences than is the case in desegregated schools.*

During the 1963-64 school year both black and white students engaged in many activities sponsored by the high school in various classes that were more social than educational. These activities included social dances of various kinds, junior-senior proms, junior-senior trips, hayrides, special parties to celebrate special events, and sociocivic events that also included laymen. Many of these activities could be clearly labeled "premating" activities. For our purposes, premating activities are those social or extracurricular activities sponsored by the school to provide teenage youth with acceptable and wholesome opportunities to interact with age mates who might be candidates for marriage. This role of the school in sponsoring premating activities was much more pronounced in smaller communities, where other recreational and social opportunities were severely limited. Often the high school represented the only facility large enough to accommodate more than a few people at one time for any social event. Without the high school, few high school students, black or white, would have been afforded the opportunity to take part in formal dances or related affairs or to take a trip to some historic setting away from home. The high school offered a social outlet for students who lived in communities that were otherwise without the means to provide this outlet.

After the onset of school desegregation in North Carolina, most premating activities sponsored by the high school disappeared immediately. Any activity that made it possible for teenagers of the opposite sex to have social contact after and during the school day were eliminated. Because of the long history of social separation between the races in North Carolina, few, if any, communities would permit the high school to sponsor any activity that increased the probability of social contact and interaction between youth at the premating stage. In the majority of communities both black and white students suffered when the high school refused to continue to sponsor social activities for all students in the community. Since most communities could not afford, or did not have the desire, to provide alternate settings for meaningful and wholesome social contact between teenage youth outside the school, students were left to their own devices in forming a social posture to fit the changing scene. In most instances the patterns worked out by the students were less acceptable than the social activities that would have resulted under the guidance and sponsorship of the school.

Social activities initiated by the students themselves immediately following school desegregation generally fell just outside the law or the moral standards of the community as a whole. There were increased instances of wild parties in isolated areas and in nightspots that bent the rules governing the serving of alcoholic beverages to underage youth. Some professional educators reported that there was also a marked increase in sexual activity. This tended to force personal relationships between students to become more permanent than might have been the case if there had been greater opportunities for them to come into social contact with a greater variety of age mates. In addition, the students' exposure to social patterns enabling them to make relevant decisions about social reality was limited. This was a definite loss for all students after school desegregation in North Carolina.

Another limitation imposed on black students after school desegregation occurred in the program areas. The example we have comes from a study of the special events "circulars" or "programs" of music (choral music, and band) and drama (plays, skits, and debate) activities that were part of the local, regional, and statewide extracurricular experiences of students in the black high school. Programs from choral music and band performances reveal that black students who participated in such extracurricular activities were exposed to and performed many types of music by many different composers. Performances included classical, popular, religious, and comic numbers. The composers of the selected works came from many different cultural backgrounds and from many different eras. Works by black composers were performed, but the majority of what was performed was not by black composers.

In dramatics, students in black high schools performed a variety of works, written by authors from different eras and cultural backgrounds, which dealt with a variety of subjects and explored the complexity of the human condition. Shakespearean works were as much candidates for performance by black students as were works written by Leroi Jones or Lorraine Hansberry. The black student in the black high school was generally exposed to a wide variety of literature covering all phases of life in America and other lands at different times and in a variety of contexts. This exposure helped many black students to broaden their experience vicariously and directly and to aspire to goals that were not inherent in their personal daily experiences in their local communities.

There is some evidence that extracurricular exposure to music and literature (includes dramatics) for black students has changed for the worse as high schools desegregate. Since many of the staff (mostly white at the present) who are responsible for extracurricular activities are not really familiar with the works of black artists and authors, they are unable to help provide black students with as balanced a diet of literary and musical works as did the black high school. As a concession to black students and their parents, many staff have permitted these students to perform only the works of blacks in literature and music without requiring that they be exposed to works by nonblacks. In short, the literary and musical works become color typed and limited to performance by specific groups of students. This practice severely limits the quality, depth, and breadth of experiences that black students are exposed to in too many desegregated school settings today. If black students' exposure continues to be limited in this way, their opportunities for choice will be limited by the fact that the school has failed to make available to them a wide range of experiences. Now that schools are desegregated, programs must realize their responsibility to extend the range of experience for a greater number of students from different backgrounds who want some of the same things from life—to share equally in the prosperity of the nation while they contribute to improving the general welfare. The school experiences each student has is critical to the direction that his life takes and to the choices he has.

Proposition 7: *Accommodation to superficial criteria limits the range, depth, and breadth of experience a student is exposed to in his program of study.*

Differences in Public Schools

Inference 8: *Catering to the ethnic and racial differences in a school creates an unmanageable and a negative view of handling desegregated schools. If pluralism is used as an organizing principle in desegregated schools, the practices that evolve are likely to have a detrimental effect on the students that are served.*

The inferences outlined above grow out of programs in desegregated schools that are designed to cater to ethnic differences and to foster the values of pluralism as manifested in cultural groups and adaptations. This is evidenced by the creation of black studies programs, black student organizations, and black performance groups within the school. In itself, this development is not a bad practice. However, the danger is always present that these practices are thought of as the *exclusive property of black students* and *for all black students.* The idea evolves and it becomes accepted that all blacks share a common ethnic and experiential background and would be interested in a program designed especially for them. Carrying the idea further, members of the school community begin to accept the idea that the presence of these special ethnic programs have taken care of all the concerns, problems, and interests of all black students attending the school. Therefore, it is concluded that there is no further need to continue to make basic changes in the structure of the school to make its services more generally available to all students.

In this way ethnic studies and activities become a trap for black students who would like to have other experiences and would like to participate in other activities. If the school atmosphere causes a student to feel that he has a special place provided apart from the general services available in the school's program, it deprives this student of the freedom of choice that is so necessary for personal growth and development. Ethnic studies and activities are a sensitive issue in desegregated schools and cause a great deal of uneasiness on both sides. To segregate students for any reason within a desegregated school is to provide them with more or less than their equal share of available educational services. As for the black student, evidence suggests that many are receiving less than their equal share of educational services because *ideology* rather than *institutional purpose* is shaping decisions related to the allocation and delivery of educational services. This is and will continue to be a crucial problem facing desegregated schools in North Carolina and throughout the country.

Proposition 8: *Special programs that cater to special groups of students divert human and material resources from the core program to activities of questionable educational value.*

Desegregation and Community in
Public High Schools

The desegregation of public high schools in North Carolina destroyed "community" within the schools for the black student specifically, and ultimately this change is likely to contribute to the destruction or at the very least, a radically altered direction for the black community in general. Destruction of community within the black high schools is, in part, related to the loss of black influence and control over the shape, kind, and extent of educational experiences black youth are to have. In addition, the desegregation of public high schools in North Carolina proved to be *school consolidation* and, as such, reduced the number of high schools (attendance units) in the state by almost one-half and increased dramatically the student population in each attendance unit. While the long-term consequences of desegregating public high schools on the lives of black youth and their communities is not known, the findings to date suggest that the loss of the black high school has had profound effects on the opportunity structure of black youth for meaningful participation and building positive self-concepts. To the extent that black youth are limited in their exposure to meaningful participation experiences that build and reinforce positive self-concepts, black individuals in particular and black communities in general experience a sharp reduction in their ability to set and achieve goals vital to their interests and concerns.

The loss of community within public high schools for black youth has had a pervasive and generally negative effect on their opportunity structure for acquiring meaningful educational and participation experiences. This situation is related to the nature of community as it refers to the public high school experience of black youth. Community in the sense it is being used here is closely related to the notion put forth by Talcott Parsons when he asserts that

Though relative territorial location inherently enters into all action it is of particularly crucial significance in two contexts. One is that of residential location. The plurality of roles of any individual actor implies a time-allocation between them, and conditions are such that the time-segments cannot be long enough to permit more than limited spatial mobility in the course of the change-over between at least some of them, e.g., family and job. This means that the main "bases of operations" of the action of an individual must be within a limited territorial area, though "commuting" by mechanical means has considerably extended the range. This base of operations requirement is at the basis of the grouping we call a "community." A community is that collectivity the members of which share a common territorial area as their base of operations for daily activities.[6]

The desegregation of public high schools removed the "base of operations" for black youth in a shared common territorial area. When the black high school ceased to exist, the "collectivity" of school membership changed. The ingroup membership ceased to exist for black youth when they no longer attended the black high school. Desegregation changed the public high school for black youth from "our" school to "their" school. The desegregated school for black youth no longer represented "a common territorial area as their base of operations for daily activities." Therefore, it was no longer possible for black youth to experience a sense of community in the desegregated high school.

The loss of the sense of community black youth had in the public high school that is intimately tied to an increase in the size of the student population in each attendance unit and the reduction of the number of participation opportunities was well documented in *Big Schools, Small Schools* by Barker and Gump.[7] In their discussion of structural characteristics of schools of different sizes, Barker and Gump assert:

We have discovered that small high schools are, in fact, not so small on the inside as they are on the outside. In terms of number of behavior settings, number of varieties of behavior settings, and number of inhabitants per setting—interior characteristics not easily seen from the outside—small schools differ less from large schools than in terms of number of students and amount of space, which are perceptually salient external attributes of schools.[8]

When small black high schools were integrated with small white high schools there were structural changes both inside and outside the larger desegregated school that exerted a different environmental press. There was a reduction in opportunities for participation both in terms of the number of behavior settings available and the number of positions that needed to be filled. Another way of viewing the problem is to point to the fact that the demand expanded for fewer resources. This study's findings to date suggest that the majority of the black youth in desegregated high schools showed a net loss when such structural changes occurred.

The work of Barker and Gump gives us further insight into the problem created for black high school students when integration gave rise to school consolidation and vastly increased student population. When these researchers looked carefully and in great detail at the actual pattern of participation that characterized small and large schools they found

clear evidence of greater participation in school activities by small school students than by large school students in all public records available to us. The differences were so great as to suggest not only that they were statistically significant differences but that they pointed to a different way of student life in a small and large school.[9]

These findings confirm our contention that changes in the size of schools resulting from desegregation altered the pattern of participation black youth experienced in the larger school setting. From the vantage point of the information gathered in this study, the change in the student life pattern experienced by black students in desegregated high schools were basically negative and nonsupportive. This situation took away opportunities for valid educational experiences from black youth who were in need of *more* such experiences rather than *less.*

One other set of findings related to small and large student schools noted by Barker and Gump deals with participation in nonclass settings. This group of relationships observed in these settings hold particular relevancy for dealing with the participation patterns of black students in public high schools before and after desegregation. The findings of Barker and Gump suggest

A large school provides a somewhat larger number and wider variety of nonclass activities than a small school. But in spite of specific large school advantages in the variety of settings, the small school makes the same general kinds of activities available to its students. Moreover, the small school provides a higher proportion of settings to the number of students; this has the following consequences for the student's participation in activities:

a. Small school students participate in the same *number* of settings commonly regarded as extracurricular as do large school students.
b. Small school students participate in a wider variety of extracurricular activities than do the students in a large school.
c. A much larger portion of small school students hold positions of importance and responsibility.
d. Finally, small school students hold responsible and central positions in a wider variety of activities than do students in a large school.[10]

Data collected on black high schools in North Carolina support the findings outlined above by Barker and Gump. Black students had few opportunities for participation in nonclass activities in the larger desegregated high schools. This is related to the fact that there were more students competing for fewer positions, specialization restricted the number of different things that any one student could do, there were fewer positions of importance available, and there was less opportunity to practice a variety of participation experiences. The larger desegregated high schools, which had a much greater student population than the all-black high schools, provided an environment that made it more difficult for black students to become that "collectivity" of members who shared a common territorial area as their base of operations for daily activities. Changes in the nature of the collectivity and the territorial area altered the black student's base of operations for daily activities in the desegregated high school. This resulted in the loss of "community" for the black student. Larger high schools created by desegregation ceased to provide the majority of black students with adequate opportunities for participation, and thereby reduced the existence of community they once experienced in their high-school experience.

The change in high school size brought about by desegregation reduced opportunities for white students to participate in school activities also. However, the negative impact was greater on the black student, because the high school represented the only opportunity for a large number of black students to participate in a number of different activities that provided meaningful practice experiences and contributed to their personal development while providing prerequisite learnings required to get involved in many attractive and necessary social functions. Because white students had access to similar participation opportunities in the larger community, the reduction in participation opportunities did not have a similar effect on their life-related experiences. The desegregation of the public high school had a differential effect on the opportunity structure of black and white students. White and black students had less opportunity to participate in school sponsored activities both in number and variety. However, the white student had alternative sources for participation opportunities and no such sources were available for the black student. The lost opportunities for meaningful participation was total and far-reaching for the black student when the public high school desegregated. This loss is likely to have negative consequences for the black student and his community, because the skills that would have been gained from participating in school activities is no longer available to a large number of black students in the public high school. Therefore this opportunity will not be available to the black student in particular and black community in general until alternate social institutions become accessible to this group for meaningful learning and practice experiences.

Since size is only one of the factors that affected the black student's feelings of community in the public high school after desegregation, some attention should be directed to the other factors mentioned earlier. The loss of black influence and control over the shape, kind, and extent of educational experiences for black youth had very negative effects on the sociological and psychological development of black youth and their respective communities. In the main there is a growing feeling that the public high school is not geared to the needs and desires of black youth. The public high school is seen as furthering the interests of the "man" (whites) at the expense of the black community. Most blacks in North Carolina now believe that the public high school can no longer be used for personal and social development in the black community. More and more the black community feels that the loss of black high school will hamper forever their chance to utilize public funds in accord with their goals for making progress on an equal basis with other groups. Without control over the direction and resources of the public high school, many members of the black community feel that they have lost the right to formulate and implement educational policy to fulfill their own self interests. In short, the black community feels that the loss of the black high school took away their ability to determine the nature of their children's education and to control the quantity and quality of experiences required for development in desired directions. The demise of the black high school in North Carolina eliminated the capability of the black community to exercise direct control over the daily implementation and operation of the educational experiences their children have. The void in the black community is unmistakable and quite painful. There is much soul searching concerning the correctness and value of the decision to *integrate* without safeguards for controlling one's destiny. Therein lies the paradox of desegregating the public high schools in North Carolina.

One last note on the loss of the black high school focuses on some of the broader opportunity costs to the black community. For one thing, fewer black students now have the opportunity to acquire leadership and apprenticeship experiences needed to prepare for personal and community development. The elimination of the black high school reduced the opportunities for professional participation and advancement for black educators with a number of different skills. Black parents have few opportunities for meaningful involvement in determining critical decisions affecting their lives and the life chances of their children. Some of the specific losses engendered by the loss of the black high school are graphically presented in the table below.

Data presented below graphically illustrate some of the statistical and factural losses the black community sustained as a result of desegregating the public schools in southern and border states. The losses in areas that are not as easily identified and quantified may represent greater and more far-reaching losses to the black community specifically and the total community generally. The latter losses will be discussed briefly later. According to data shown in the table, 31,584 black teachers were displaced by discriminatory hiring and dismissals in relation to the percentage of black students on basis of a teacher/pupil ratio of approximately 1 to 24. The money loss to individual teachers was great and personally unacceptable, but the aggregate money loss of the black communities in the states in question was staggering for 1970. If this aggregate loss were projected over the four school years that have transpired since 1970, the public money directed away from the black community in the form of teachers' salaries amounts to more than one billion dollars. This loss in public money to the black community means that the black citizens of these states are not getting their share of tax moneys intended for public educational institutions, and black businessmen and other skilled workmen were deprived of the opportunity to provide services to a group of black professionals that had been available to them in past years. When the black community in seventeen of the poorest states is asked to sustain a billion dollar loss in salary over a four-year period, the direct and indirect consequences of such an act is likely to have negative effects many years to come. In terms of compounding the interests on capital (black teacher's salary), the black community in these states may never recover the loss.

If one were to compute the loss of income the black community incurred in 1973 in North Carolina, there were approximately one hundred fewer principals than would have been expected prior to the desegregation of black high schools. (In 1973, there were 366 high schools in North Carolina. During the 1963-64

Table 7-1
Employment and Dollar Loss for Black Educators in Seventeen Southern and Border States

State	Total Pupils 1970	Total Teachers 1970	Pupil Teacher Ratio	Number of Black Students	Expected No. of Black Teachers Under Singleton Number of Degree/Based On Pupil Teacher Ratio	Actual Number of Black Teachers 1970	Percent Difference	Number of Black Teachers Displaced by Discriminatory Hiring and Dismissals	Average Teacher Salary 1970	Cost Black Communities in Dollars 1970
Alabama	780,286	31,279	25	268,593	10,744	9,452	12	1,292	6,954	8,984,568
Arkansas	368,035	15,299	25	107,213	4,289	3,121	27	1,168	6,445	7,527,760
Delaware	128,735	5,570	23	26,438	1,149	804	30	345	9,300	3,208,500
Florida	1,436,487	59,648	24	332,121	13,838	11,340	18	2,498	8,600	25,482,800
Georgia	1,099,446	43,818	25	364,868	14,595	12,236	16	2,359	7,372	17,390,548
Kentucky	654,711	26,672	25	61,473	2,459	1,287	47	1,172	7,624	8,935,328
Louisiana	841,656	35,184	24	340,447	14,188	12,145	14	2,040	7,220	14,728,800
Maryland	911,618	37,344	25	220,166	8,807	7,252	17	1,555	9,885	15,371,175
Mississippi	533,289	22,301	24	271,932	11,331	9,163	19	2,168	6,012	13,034,016
Missouri	857,890	35,607	24	141,005	5,875	3,645	37	2,230	8,091	18,042,930
N. Carolina	1,187,048	47,221	25	351,182	14,047	10,996	21	3,051	7,744	23,626,944
Oklahoma	455,754	18,656	24	47,720	1,988	1,400	29	588	7,139	4,197,732
S. Carolina	640,148	25,746	25	262,974	10,519	8,482	19	2,037	7,000	14,259,000
Tennessee	877,778	33,625	26	188,754	7,260	5,724	21	1,536	7,290	11,197,440
Texas	2,468,283	105,186	23	398,187	17,312	12,672	26	4,640	7,503	34,813,920
Virginia	1,067,292	45,489	23	258,280	11,230	8,498	24	2,732	8,200	22,402,400
W. Virginia	392,690	16,223	24	18,972	791	618	21	173	7,850	1,358,050
Totals	14,701,036	604,868	N/A	3,660,322	150,419	118,835		31,584		244,561,911

Source: John W. Smith and Betty M. Smith, "For Black Educators: Integration Brings the Axe," *The Urban Review*, vol. 6, no. 3, 1973, p. 8. Reprinted by permission of APS Publications.

scholastic year 31 percent of all of the high school principals in North Carolina were black. On that basis there should have been about 114 black principals in the state in 1973. There were only fifteen black high school principals in 1973.) Since principals in North Carolina earned approximately $13,000 annually, the public money loss to the black community in North Carolina amounted to more than $1,300,000 in 1973. When this amount is coupled with the public money loss in teachers' salaries of more than 24 million dollars, the black community in North Carolina sustained a public money loss of more than 25 million dollars in 1973. In the writer's estimation this loss will not be recovered by the black community in North Carolina.

It is readily apparent that the black community in North Carolina sustained vast economic losses when they were denied direct access to public funds in the form of educational salaries after schools were desegregated. The findings of this study suggest that this loss is likely to become larger in the immediate future. This loss has lessened the black community's ability to attract funds into its coffers for development and long-term growth. Since it is questionable if income from other sources will ever make up the deficit that was created by the displacement of black educational personnel in North Carolina in particular and in other southern and border states in general, the black community in these areas has been handed one more handicap in addition to the array of problems they face. Under these conditions any progress made by the black community is well deserved and surely earned.

One last note about the loss sustained by the black community resulting from integration refers to broader areas that are not easily documented and described. These areas refer to the social and psychological factors that affect the will, confidence, and positive outlook of black citizens. The loss of the black high school has placed great strain on cohesiveness of the black community. As cohesiveness is eroded, the sense of community that sustained black people in their darkest hours is lessened to a dangerous degree. As the *politics of integration* take hold there will be a greater demand for a strong "source of community" among the black population if they are to achieve the level of organization and participation necessary to gain their fair share of resources for self-determination and development. Without such a cohesive force in the black community as our society moves toward integration, it is doubtful if meaningful and effective political decisions will be directed toward the black community to deal with the many social problems made hard and resistant to solution through years of neglect. That is the challenge to the black community in southern states in particular and all states in general in the immediate future.

Now that the black high school is no longer available to the black community as a positive force for self-determination and development, other social institutions must take its place. The opportunities that were provided by the black high school for black youth, educators, parents and laymen must continue to be available to the black community even to a greater degree than when the influence of the black high school was at its height. If the activities conducted by the black high school are not made available to members of the black population, it is doubtful if "community" will be sustained at a level necessary for achieving important individual and social goals. The form and nature of the social institution that is likely to evolve to replace the contributions and services of the black high school has not appeared as yet, even though the need is readily apparent. The fate of the black community might well rest on its ability to replace the services rendered by the black high school.

The black community paid, is paying, and will likely continue to pay the price for public school desegregation. There are many questions with which the black community must deal. One of the primary questions facing the black community is concerned with whether or not desegregation represents a net gain or loss. Another way to put the question is will the seed of integration grow into a strong tree that bears good social fruit or will the investment in pure economic terms and social upheaval pay dividends greater than would have been the case under segregation? Other important questions:

1. How do you provide meaningful practice and participation opportunities for black youth?

2. How do you organize a community for social action when it has no integrative, pervasive social institution?

3. How do you assess the impact of policy and practice changes on a community as a collective or on individuals that comprise it?

4. How do you communicate the negative feelings of a community that are brought about by changes in policy and practice? and

5. How do you alert professional educators to real changes in opportunity costs resulting from changes in policy and practice?

The fate of the black community may very well rest on the answers that are generated in response to the above questions. Much is at stake for all the citizens in America and in other countries. We must find creative and meaningful answers to the questions facing the black community that result from the desegregation of public schools in the South and other states.

Appendixes

Appendix A:
Methods Used to Describe
the Black High School

Historical Perspective

A brief look at the development of public education in North Carolina points up the unique development of black high schools in that state. For resources, there are the studies of Marcus C.S. Noble's *A History of the Public Schools of North Carolina* and several chapters in Louis R. Harlan's *Separate and Unequal.* State records on salaries, capital expenditures, sources of funding, etc., dating from 1873 (when for all intents and purposes public schooling for blacks began and white public schools opened again on a full scale for the first time since the Civil War) provide much of the support for many of the observations in this book. Except for Harlan's book, there is little on North Carolina schools in the 1900-1915 period. During the 1920s North Carolina became really concerned with high school education and the quality of schooling, and the state began inquiring more into the situation. The conditions, especially in the rural schools, both black and white, caused great concern, and consolidation (of white schools) became common.

For the 1930s, studies such as that commissioned by Governor Ehringhaus in 1933, *Three Hundred Years of American High Schools*, provide material on the black high school, and for the 1940s other studies by the North Carolina Education Commission, such as *Education in North Carolina Today and Tomorrow*, were extremely useful in conjunction with the biennial reports issued every other year since 1882 by the Office of State Superintendent on Public Instruction. Information for the fifties is drawn from these biennial reports and from several studies done as a result of the 1954 *Brown v. Board of Education* desegregation decision by the U.S. Supreme Court.

State Data

As noted above, state data, collected fairly regularly since 1873-74, proved to be crucial to the analysis. But because the main interest was in looking at the black high school at a specific point in time, most of the focus was on the raw detailed information the schools reported to the Department of Public Instruction each year. There were, however, several problems. Perhaps the most difficult task was finding out what data were available and where they were located. Data are not kept by school but by year, by county, and by administrative unit within each county for information gathered each year, such as individual school enrollment. However, all data gathered along these lines are not necessarily kept in one place, so that data were found on school enrollment in the Management Information Systems section of the Office of Public Instruction and in the Preliminary and Annual Reports issued by each school in the state archives.

Other information, not collected annually, was filed by county and administrative unit within the county, and such folders may contain information gathered over a period, say, of thirty years. This was particularly the case with information on school opening dates. Some of the information received came from the Office of Public Instruction's Division of School Planning and that data did not cover all schools. A considerable amount of information was obtained from people in the Division of Secondary Education and in the Research and Development Area. Basically there were two problems with collecting state data:

1. Although people might know all there was to know about the information their departments had, they usually were not informed as to what data other departments had. This was a result of a decentralized data system.

2. There was no single place where all possible information on each school was stored. Furthermore, data were not arranged by school.

On the whole, official data obtained from local administrative units proved of little help, owing to the nature of their record keeping, the changes in personnel occurring since schools were integrated, the cautiousness of administrators in dealing with racially related material, and the logistical problems involved in obtaining information from overworked staff, who were expected to locate, package, and mail the material to the writer.

The State Department discontinued the practice of collecting separate data on black and white schools at the close of the 1963-64 school year. It was therefore decided that that year should serve as the boundary line period for collecting, collating, analyzing, summarizing, and evaluating the data that described the black high school as a dynamic operating unit. Since 1963-64 is the year for which the latest data for the greatest number of black high schools was available, it was felt that data generated during this year would present the most accurate and recent record of its functions, activities, opportunities, limitations, and the beliefs affecting its operational efforts as a unique institution in the history of American education.

Unofficial Data

State figures, however, tell only part of the story, the quantitative aspects of the black high school. Certainly as important, if not more so, is the information on the qualitative aspects of the black high school. To obtain this information attention was focused on those most deeply involved with the schools. This group included principals, superintendents, teachers, students, parents, and community leaders.

Of course this part of the analysis is the most problematic, for two reasons.

First, the focus of attention was on an institution that no longer existed: the black high school in a dual school system. Those who reported their experiences were looking back with hindsight, and, as we are all aware, time can be a selective filter. This does not invalidate what they said, but it does make it necessary to corroborate as many different people's version of the way it was, so as to provide as accurate a general picture as possible. The second problem is the danger that those dealing with qualitative information will either unintentionally misinterpret it, because they are not familiar with the background against which the information must be seen, or that they will intentionally manipulate the information to reinforce their particular point of view. In dealing with the first problem of interpretation an attempt was made to offer as a remedy historical data and as much quantitative data as could be found to give the proper perspective. In this case, the long-time perspective of our principal investigator became the critical factor. Insofar as the second problem of interpretation is concerned, again there was an attempt to avoid criticism by providing as much quantitative information as could be obtained. There was an effort to temper the view of the high school, which was gained mainly from those on the inside, by interviewing superintendents, all of whom were white and all of whom said that although they had regular but infrequent dealings with the black high school principal, they were not too involved with the black high school, especially in its day-to-day functioning and its social role in the black community.

Data were obtained for qualitative information in two ways: questionnaires and interviews.

Questionnaires

These were administered to five groups of people: principals, teachers and special staff, parents, students, and community leaders.

Principals

The questionnaires sent to principals covered several areas of school operation. They solicited information on the principal's background, the background of the student body, the school, extracurricular activities, and information on how active students were in such activities.

Teachers and Special Staff

These questionnaires, rather than just being sent out, were administered by project staff using a structured questionnaire. All those questioned (twenty-five) had worked in black high schools. They were mainly questioned as to the extent that black high school students participated in such activities as band, choir, athletics, and any other extracurricular activities.

Parents

The twenty-five parents to whom questionnaires were administered had all had children who attended black high schools at some time. The primary concern here was with what parents felt the role of the school had been in the community, but we also wanted to know how involved parents had been in such school-related organizations as the PTA, Boosters' Clubs, etc.

Students

As in the case of the teachers, questionnaires were administered by project staff. The fifty students who participated had attended all-black high schools at least some of the time they had been in high school. The students provided information on the way they felt about their school and about the kinds of relationships they had had with their teachers.

Community Leaders

The ten community leaders consisted of local ministers and elected officials, such as city council members (although in 1963-64 none had actually held official positions, so that at that time these men were just those who had been respected within the community). As with the parents, community leaders were questioned as to what they perceived to have been the role of the black high school in the community.

Interviews

Nothing quite makes up for person-to-person discussions in trying to capture the flavor of an experience. Questionnaires do not elicit answers to unasked questions, and they rarely provide for elaboration of what might turn out to be complex questions. But the interviewer is free to follow up some chance mention of an event, and in forming, even if very brief, some sort of relationship with those being interviewed, he can often elicit much more complete explanations than any questionnaire can. Interviews were conducted with those who had been principals in black high schools and superintendents whose administrative units included black high schools. Most interviews with the principal were taped, and most lasted for an hour, although there were some two-hour sessions. Taped interviews were then transcribed in full and subjected to a simplified content analysis. Some interviews with superintendents were taped (and these, too, were transcribed in full), but most were not. The interviewer took notes and wrote up the interview as soon after the event as practicable.

Principals

Twenty principals were interviewed on how they ran their schools, on what sorts of duties were required of them by law, and what they actually had to do. This last point provided the main theme of the interviews. They were also queried as to the role they themselves and their schools played in community life.

Superintendents

Twenty superintendents were interviewed, mainly with an eye to putting the role of the black high school and the black high school principal in the perspective of the larger community. We were particularly interested in finding out whether superintendents knew what black principals were up to and whether or not they were aware of the roles, other than that required by law, that the black principal chose to play or was forced to play.

Appendix B:
Statistical Survey of Black
High School in 1963-64

The three major sources of information for data presented are the *Biennial Report of The Superintendent of Public Instruction of North Carolina* (for the scholastic years 1962-63 and 1963-64, Part One), *Educational Directory 1963-64*, and *North Carolina State Department of Public Instruction Final Enrollment Tally for the 1963-64 Scholastic Year.* Even though some minor discrepancies in official data sources do exist, they do not alter the basic picture of the black high school in North Carolina.

Summary of Findings

1. Black people comprised 24.5 percent and 22.2 percent of the total state population in 1960 and 1970 respectively.

2. The percentage of blacks in 1960 across all counties ranged from none to 62.6 percent.

3. Half of all counties in 1960 had a percentage of black people that was larger than the percentage (24.5 percent) of blacks living in the state.

4. In 1963-64 funds for supporting public schools came from three major sources: state (78.4 percent), local (17.4 percent), and federal (4.2 percent).

5. More than 75 percent of the state funds for school support came from income and sales taxes, and at the local level more than 75 percent of funds came from property taxes and bonds in 1963-64.

6. In twenty-seven out of thirty-one state budget expenditure items, black staff and schools received a larger percentage (ranging from 25 percent to 38 percent) of the budget than their proportional representation (24.5 percent in 1960) in the total state population.

7. In the majority of instances (twenty-eight state budget expenditure items), black staff and schools received a smaller percentage of the funds than the percentage (31 percent) black high schools represented of the total number of high schools in the state in 1963-64.

8. In all but one instance (thirty state budget expenditure items), black staff and schools received a smaller percentage of the funds than the percentage (36 percent) black student enrollment represented of the total number of high school students enrolled in 1963-64.

9. There were 226 regular black high schools (24 senior, 23 junior-senior, 179 Union, grades 1-12) in the state in 1963-64. There were 250 black public schools with high school grades.

10. Of the counties (ninety-one) with black schools, 44 percent of the

counties had only one black high school and 46.2 percent had two to four black high schools. Only a small percentage of the counties had more.

11. The majority (70.7 percent) of the administrative units (140 in number) with black high schools had only one black high school. Only 20.7 percent of the counties had two to three black high schools, with few having more.

12. Of the seventy-two high schools for which we had opening dates, more than half (54.1 percent) of them were opened before 1930, 11.2 percent of them opened after 1945, and the remaining 34.7 percent were opened between 1930 and 1945.

13. There were 85,948 black high school students enrolled, and they comprised 36 percent of the total state enrollment in 1963-64 in public high schools.

14. On the basis of enrollment and average daily attendance, black high schools had an average of 380 and 333 students per high school, respectively.

15. The average daily attendance of black high school students was 75,290, which represented 34.6 percent of the total average daily attendance for the state in 1963-64.

16. More than half (55.4 percent) of all black high schools enrolled fewer than three hundred students, and 10.3 percent of them enrolled more than six hundred students in 1963-64.

17. Black high schools had a larger percentage of ninth-graders, which reflects the corresponding lower percentage of enrollment in eleventh and twelfth grades in 1963-64.

18. The average daily attendance in 1963-64 in black high schools was 91.8 percent of the average daily membership.

19. The average number of days attended per black high school student in 1963-64 was 166 days per student out of a required number of 180 days.

20. Only about 67 percent of those black students who entered ninth grade graduated from high school four years later. The percentage of whites completing high school is only slightly higher.

21. The average daily absences for black high school students was 7.6 percent of the average daily enrollment in 1963-64.

22. There were 12,964 black high school graduates, comprising 24.4 percent of the total number of graduates in the state in 1963-64.

23. A large percentage of black high school graduates enrolled in colleges (26.8 percent) and postsecondary schools (7.2 percent) in 1963-64.

24. Most black graduates (61.3 percent) went to work immediately following graduation in 1963-64. Only 42.4 percent of white graduates fell into this category.

25. There were 3401 black high school teachers, comprising 24.8 percent of all the high school teachers in the state in 1963-64.

26. There were 226 black high school principals, comprising 30.3 percent of all staff so categorized in 1963-64.

27. Almost all (99 percent) black teachers in 1963-64 held the highest certificate status (Class A and/or Graduate) required for their position and for continued employment.

28. The majority (86.1 percent) of black principals in 1963-64 held the highest certificate (Class A and Graduate) status required for their position and for continued employment.

29. All black supervisors in 1963-64 held the highest certificate status (Class A and/or Graduate) required for their position and for continued employment.

30. The average annual salary in 1963-64 for black high school teachers ($5030.23) was higher than that of white high school teachers.

31. The average annual salary in 1963-64 for black principals and supervisors ($8950.85) was higher than that of whites in similar positions.

32. The average annual salary in 1963-64 for black vocational teachers ($6269.67) was lower than that of whites holding similar positions.

33. Of the 226 black high schools, 211 (93.4 percent) were accredited by the state of North Carolina and 49 (21.7 percent) were approved by the Southern Association.

34. Of the seventy-two black high schools for which we have opening dates, twenty-eight (38.8 percent) were accredited within the first five years of operation, and more than half (61.0 percent) during the first ten years of operation. A little less than one quarter (22.3 percent) of these schools required more than fifteen years to receive accreditation.

35. Most (72.1 percent) black high schools had been accredited for more than twenty years. The mean number of years senior, junior-senior and union high schools had been accredited was thirty years, thirty-one years and twenty-four years, respectively.

36. Black high schools offered eleven out of twelve of all the English subjects offered in the state, all of the mathematics subjects, all of the science subjects, all of the trades and industries subjects, all of the music subjects, all of the art subjects, all of the industrial arts and education subjects, all of the physical education subjects, all of the Bible subjects, all of the psychology subjects (1), fourteen out of seventeen foreign language subjects, all of the business education subjects, four out of five agriculture subjects, all of the social studies subjects, five out of six of the home economics subjects, two out of four of the industrial cooperative training subjects, and two out of three distributive education subjects.

37. The number of black schools offering specific courses varied widely in the major subject areas. In the English area, there was one course that was offered by 244 schools, and one course that no black school offered; in mathematics, as many as 244 schools offered one course, and one course was offered by as few as eleven schools; in science, as many as 232 schools offered one course, and there were three courses each of which was offered by only two schools; in foreign languages, as many as 230 schools offered one course, and three courses were

each offered by only one school; in business education, as many as 214 schools offered one course and one course was offered by nine schools; in the agriculture and home economics areas there was a more even distribution of offerings; and in social studies, as many as 219 schools offered one course; and one course was offered at ten schools.

38. The uneven pattern of course offerings across the state indicates that only a very small percentage of black high school students had the opportunity to select other courses in addition to those which fulfilled the basic requirements.

39. There were 190 black high school librarians comprising 27.1 percent of all high school librarians in the state in 1963-64.

40. The average amount of money allocated per student for libraries for black students in two-thirds of the black high schools was less than the $3.99 allocated per pupil for the state as a whole.

41. Of the 226 black high schools, 224 and 142 fielded boys and girls basketball teams respectively in 1963-64.

42. There were eighty-eight, seventy-five, and eighty-one black high schools with football, baseball, and track and field teams, respectively, in 1963-64.

43. Two black high schools had golf teams and sixteen had tennis teams in 1963-64.

44. No black high school had a wrestling, cross country, swimming, or soccer team.

Appendix C:
Historical Survey of the
Black High School

1823 — The North Carolina legislature passed a law authorizing the state treasurer to issue treasury notes. The proceeds were to be used to establish a permanent school fund for statewide common schools.

1825 — Literary Fund Law was passed. Its purpose was to provide support for public schools for whites.

1836 — The United States Congress ruled that any surplus left in the United States Treasury on January 1, 1837 was to be distributed to states on the basis of population and was to be used for public schools.

1838 — North Carolina State Senator H.G. Spruill proposed a resolution to provide public education to all children (whites), rich and poor.

1839 — In January the first free common school law was passed in North Carolina. In August the first school tax bill was passed, the first time around, to provide "free countywide common schools at public expense."

1854 — The Code of 1854 required that the master or mistress of white apprentices provide them with an education covering reading, writing, and basic arithmetic.

1857 — There were 3,500 school districts each with at least one schoolhouse and 150,000 of the 200,000 school age children were enrolled.
  — There were 2,256 certified teachers, 214 of whom were women.

1866 — A law was passed changing the Code of 1854 to include providing an education for all apprentices, black or white. Until then it had been a misdemeanor to teach a black to read and write.

1868 — A resolution was passed which stated that the "interests and happiness" of blacks and whites would be best served by establishing separate schools.
  — W.J.T. Hayes, a black North Carolina legislator, was appointed Assistant State Superintendent of Public Instruction, the first black appointed to such an office in any state.

1868-73 — Because of the general poverty in the South after the Civil War, little was done in the period immediately following the war to support public schools for either race.

1873 — The first publicly supported black schools came into existence in the school year 1873-74, attended by 55,000 black children representing 32 percent of all school children. At that time about 34 percent of the children between the ages of six and twenty-one were black.

1886-1902 — Black teachers' salaries were only about 10 percent lower than white teachers'.

1900 — The Democrats returned to power and Charles B. Aycock, a proponent of "universal" education, was elected governor.

— A constitutional amendment was passed which essentially disfranchised blacks.

— 50 percent more was spent on educating the white child than on the black child.

1907 — The High School Law was passed. Until then only cities and large towns had public high schools.

1914 — The first three black public high schools opened.

1915 — 300 percent more money was spent on educating the white child than on the black child.

1919 — The first black public high schools were accredited. There were four of them.

1921 — A Division of Negro Education was established in the State Department of Public Instruction.

1923 — The first black public high schools run by city or county school administrative units received accreditation.

1924 — There were fourteen accredited black public high schools.

— Few black children were able to get a high school education.

— The average educational level for black teachers was four years of high school and for white teachers about a year and a half of college.

1933 — There were 106 black public high schools, but a majority of counties still had no way to provide a high school education for their black school children.

— On the average, black teachers had about two years of college and whites about three and three quarter years of college.

1935 — A Governor's Commission published a report at the request of the governor recommending that the level of black and white schools be equalized and especially that black teachers' salaries be raised to the level of whites.

1937-48 – The educational level of white teachers dropped because of higher-paying employment in other fields.

1940 – Money spent on educating each black child was 35 percent less than that spent on each white child.

1944 – North Carolina passed a law equalizing black and white teacher salary schedules.

1945 – The conditions in black schools were still much worse than in white schools. 60 percent of black high school children were attending schools below accreditation standards.

1950 – North Carolina continued to spend more money on its black school children. 15 percent less was spent educating each black child than each white child. This was an increase in expenditures of 20 percent from 1940.

   – Black teachers' educational preparation surpassed that of whites.
   – Black teachers spent an average of 4.1 years in college and whites an average of 3.9.

1954 – The United States Supreme Court ruled that "Separate educational facilities were inherently unequal."

1957 – Charlotte, Greensboro, and Winston-Salem made an attempt to desegregate according to a pupil placement plan. However, very little was changed under this plan.

1960 – North Carolina, in an effort to retain separate schools for blacks and whites, voted in private school laws setting up "free" private schools, school closing laws, and retained pupil placement laws.

Notes

Notes

Chapter 1
Segregation, Desegregation, and
Integration in Public Schools

1. The basic data for this book was gathered in North Carolina, but the implications derived refer to all states that had legally constituted dual school systems. In addition, the references that result from these data have general utility for understanding many of the problems and practices affecting the public education of black youth in the South and in other parts of the country.

2. Charles S. Johnson, *Patterns of Negro Segregation* (New York: Harper, 1943). In *A Guide to the Study of the United States of America*, Superintendent of Documents, U.S. Government Printing Office, Washington, D.C., 1960, p. 564.

3. "Participation and Alienation," *Toward a Social Report* (Ann Arbor: University of Michigan Press, 1970), p. 79.

4. Sidney Verba, "Democratic Participation," *The Annals* 373 (September 1967): 54.

5. Ibid., p. 54.

6. Ibid., p. 54.

7. Ibid., p. 80.

8. Ibid.

Chapter 2
Purpose of the Study

1. Seventy-three percent of the total population, 72.4 percent of the white population, and 80.7 percent of the black population, according to the 1970 census, were urban dwellers. Of the 153 largest cities of 100,000 or more, 92 percent had a larger percentage of black dwellers than in the total population, fifty-three had twice the percentage, twenty-five had thrice the percentage, and four had a black population of 50 percent or more. The combined population of these cities had 55.7 percent of the total population in the United States.

2. Lowry Nelson, Charles E. Ramsey, and Coolie Verner, *Community Structure and Change* (New York: The Macmillan Co., 1960), p. 344.

Chapter 3
A Historical Perspective

1. Marcus C.S. Noble, *A History of the Public Schools of North Carolina* (Chapel Hill: University of North Carolina Press, 1930), p. 43.

2. Ibid.

3. Ibid., p. 46.

4. Ibid., p. 49.

5. Ibid., p. 54.

6. Ibid.

7. Ibid., p. 71.

8. Ibid., p. 223.

9. Ibid., p. 272.

10. Ibid., p. 273.

11. Ibid.

12. Ibid., p. 274.

13. Ibid., p. 290-91.

14. Ibid.

15. Ibid.

16. Ibid., p. 297.

17. Ibid., p. 309.

18. Ibid., p. 324.

19. Series D603-617 "Average Annual Earnings in all Industries and in Selected Industries and Occupations," *Historical Statistics of the United States: Colonial Times to 1957* (Washington, D.C.: U.S. Bureau of the Census, 1960), p. 91.

20. Louis R. Harlan, *Separate and Unequal* (New York: Atheneum, 1968), p. 105.

21. *1635-1935: Three Hundred Years of American High Schools*, State Superintendent of Public Instruction (Raleigh, N.C., 1935), p. 14.

22. *Report of the Superintendent of Public Instruction*, 1924, p. 29.

23. *Separate and Unequal*, p. 131.

24. *1635-1935: Three Hundred Years of American High Schools*, pp. 26-28.

25. *Report of Superintendent of Public Instruction*, p. 32.

26. *1635-1935: Three Hundred Years of American High Schools*, State Superintendent of Public Instruction, Raleigh, North Carolina, 1935, p. 26.

27. *Report of the Superintendent of Public Instruction*, p. 31.

28. Ibid., p. 42.

29. *Public Education in North Carolina* (New York: General Education Board, 1921), p. ix.

30. *1635-1935: Three Hundred Years of American High Schools*, pp. 37-39.

31. Ibid., pp. 37-39.

32. Ibid., p. 25.

33. Ibid., p. 43.

34. *Education in North Carolina Today and Tomorrow: Report of the State Education Commission*, p. 251.

35. Ibid.

36. Ibid., p. 252.

37. Ibid., p. 249-50.

38. Virgil A. Clift, "The History of Racial Segregation in American Education," in *The Countdown on Segregated Education* (New York: Society for the Advancement of Education, Inc., 1960), pp. 35-36.

39. Harry S. Ashmore, *The Negro and the Schools* (Chapel Hill: University of North Carolina Press, 1954), p. 153.

40. Ibid.

41. Ibid., p. 107.

42. Herbert Wey and John Corey, *Action Patterns in School Desegregation* (Bloomington, Ind.: Phi Delta Kappa, Inc., 1959), pp. 122-24.

43. Clift, p. 165.

44. Ashmore, p. 153.

Chapter 7
Inferences and Propositions for
Further Study

1. This problem is well documented and treated in a report published by the Southern Regional Council and the Robert F. Kennedy Memorial. The document is entitled *The Student Pushout: Victim of Continued Resistance to Desegregation.* It is *must* reading for anyone who is trying to understand what has been happening to black youth outside the South for a number of years and what is beginning to happen to blacks in the South at the present time during their high school experience. The conditions facing black youth today in many high schools suggest that the black community is under attack again at its very core.

2. *The Student Pushout: Victim of Continued Resistance to Desegregation*, p. 12.

3. Ibid., pp. 13-14.

4. Ibid., p. 14.

5. Roger G. Barker and Paul V. Gump, *Big School, Small School: High School Size and Student Behavior* (Stanford: Stanford University Press, 1964).

6. Talcott Parsons, *The Social System* (New York: The Free Press, 1964), p. 9.

7. Roger G. Barker and Paul V. Gump, *Big School, Small School: High School Size and Student Behavior* (Stanford, Calif.: Stanford University Press, 1964).

8. Ibid., p. 62-63.

9. Ibid., p. 74.

10. Ibid., p. 92-93.

Bibliography

Bibliography

Ashmore, Harry S. *The Negro and the Schools.* Chapel Hill: The University of North Carolina Press, 1954.

Barker, Roger G. and Paul V. Gump. *Big School, Small School: High School Size and Student Behavior.* Stanford, Calif.: Stanford University Press, 1964.

Biennial Report of the Superintendent of Public Instruction of North Carolina For the Scholastic Years 1900-1901 and 1901-1902. J.Y. Joyner, Superintendent Public Instruction. Raleigh, N.C.: Edwards and Broughton, 1902.

Biennial Report of the Superintendent of Public Instruction of North Carolina, For the Scholastic Years 1936-1937 and 1937-1938. Issued by the State Superintendent of Public Instruction, Raleigh, N.C.

Biennial Report of the Superintendent of Public Instruction of North Carolina, For the Scholastic Years 1938-1939 and 1939-1940. Issued by the State Superintendent of Public Instruction, Raleigh, N.C.

Biennial Report of the Superintendent of Public Instruction of North Carolina, For the Scholastic Years 1946-1947 and 1947-1948. Issued by the State Superintendent of Public Instruction, Raleigh, N.C.

Biennial Report of the Superintendent of Public Instruction of North Carolina, For the Scholastic Years 1948-1949 and 1949-1950. Issued by the State Superintendent of Public Instruction, Raleigh, N.C.

Brickman, William W. and Stanley Lehrer. *The Countdown on Segregated Education,* New York: Society for the Advancement of Education, 1960.

Education in North Carolina Today and Tomorrow. Members of the State Education Commission, The United Forces for Education, Raleigh, N.C., December 1948.

Harlan, Louis R. *Separate and Unequal.* New York: Atheneum, 1968.

Historical Statistics of the United States: Colonial Times to 1957, Series D603-617 "Average Annual Earnings in all Industries and in Selected Industries and Occupations." Washington, D.C.: U.S. Bureau of the Census, 1960.

Nelson, Lowry, Charles E. Ramsey, and Coolie Verner. *Community Structure and Change.* New York: The Macmillan Company, 1960.

Noble, Marcus C.S., *A History of the Public Schools of North Carolina.* Chapel Hill: University of North Carolina Press, 1930.

Parsons, Talcott. *The Social System.* New York: The Free Press, 1964.

Paul, James C.N., *Law and Government, The School Segregation Decision.* Chapel Hill: Institute of Government, The University of North Carolina, 1954.

Report and Recommendations of The Commission to Study Public Schools and Colleges for Colored People in North Carolina. Authorized by the General Assembly in Resolution No. 28, March 10, 1937, and appointed by Governor Clyde R. Hoey. State Capitol, Raleigh, N.C.

The Student Pushout: Victim of Continued Resistance to Desegregation. Atlanta: Southern Regional Council and The Robert F. Kennedy Memorial, 1973.

Wey, Herbert and John Corey. *Action Patterns in School Desegregation, A Guidebook.* Bloomington, Ind.: Phi Delta Kappa, Incorporated, 1959.

1635-1935: Three Hundred Years of American High Schools. State Superintendent of Public Instruction, Raleigh, N.C., 1935.

1956 Extra Session Laws General Assembly of North Carolina, Proposed Constitutional Amendment and Implementing Acts Relating to Public Education. Published as authorized and directed by Resolution No. 6, Issued by Thad Eure, Secretary of State, Raleigh, N.C., 1956.

Index

About the Author

Frederick A. Rodgers completed his undergraduate studies at Fayetteville State University, North Carolina, in 1960, and received the Ph.D. in Education in 1966 at the University of Illinois. Dr. Rodgers has had varied experiences teaching, including associate professorships in elementary education at New York University (1966-1970) and at the University of Illinois, from the summer of 1970 to the present. He has also held several administrative directorships in teacher education programs, and has been an educational consultant, primarily in the New York City area.

Dr. Rodgers edited the *Research Supplement* and "Research in Review" column in *Educational Leadership* (Journal of ASCD, NEA), and he has published numerous articles in professional journals. A recent text by Dr. Rodgers will be published in 1975 by Macmillan Company entitled *Curriculum and Instruction in the Elementary School.*